insparation

A TEEN'S GUIDE TO HEALTHY LIVING INSPIRED BY TODAY'S TOP SPAS

Mary Beth Sammons and Samantha Moss

Illustrations by Azadeh Houshyar

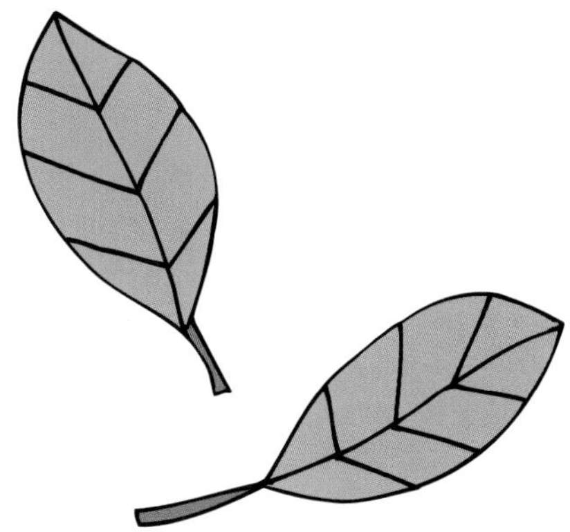

Watson-Guptill Publications/New York

First published in 2005 by
Watson-Guptill Publications,
a division of VNU Business Media, Inc.
770 Broadway, New York, NY 10003
www.wgpub.com

Created and produced by Watson-Guptill Publications and Orange Avenue Publishing, San Francisco, CA

Text set in Gill Sans; cover and accent text set in Wunderlich; quote text set in BauerBodoni

Library of Congress Control Number: 2005922538
ISBN: 0-8230-2641-8

CREDITS
Senior Acquisitions Editor/Watson-Guptill: Julie Mazur
Editor/Watson-Guptill: Anne McNamara

Creative Directors
Tanya Napier and Hallie Warshaw

Writers
Mary Beth Sammons: Spa treatment text and spa descriptions
Samantha Moss: At-home treatments
Deborah Burkman: At-home treatments (Yoga, Meditative Walk, Zen Zone-In, Chakra Chanting, Deep De-Stress)
Erin Conley: Main book introduction, chapter introductions, and back cover text

Illustrator
Azadeh Houshyar

Graphic Designers
Tanya Napier and Hallie Warshaw

Editor
Vicky Elliott

Production Artist
Doug Popovich

Photos
Courtesy of the spas

Printed in China.
First printing, 2005
1 2 3 4 5 6 7 8 / 12 11 10 09 08 07 06 05

insparation

cleanser

Yogurt

INTRODUCTION

Spas and resorts used to be just for adults—but no longer! All over the country, the hottest spas are catering to a hip new clientele: health- and beauty-conscious teens, just like you. This is great news, for sure, but what if your after-school job isn't earning quite enough cash for that oh-so-glamorous spa retreat? Or what if your last visit to a spa left you wanting more, more, more? That's where we come in.

InSPAration is your very own insider's guide to the good life. Inspired by actual teen treatments from more than 30 spas, it's packed with do-it-yourself treats for everything from facials to fitness, beauty to ballet, meditation to makeup. The six themed sections take a total-body approach to looking and feeling great, with helpful tips from the pros and deluxe treatments to get you glowing inside and out. Read the book from cover to cover, or pick and choose treatments based on whatever you need at any given moment.

Get comfortable in your own skin and face the world with a radiant complexion in **Skin Smoothers.** **Body Builders** will help you take the work out of workouts and make the most of your natural assets. Want to give your look a lift? Go from humdrum to hot stuff with the cool ideas in **Beauty Boosters.** If life's got you frazzled and frayed, tune in to your needs and tone down the pace with **Stress Zappers.** Feeling the blues? Let out your inner sparkle and humor your heart with **Spirit Lifters.** Or, why not give the gift of glamour to your closest friends by hosting your very own spa party? We've got something for everyone who wants to feel fabulous, face to foot, and it's all right here at your fingertips!

It's time to stop imagining the good life and start living it. So go on:

Get pampered.

Get healthy.

Get inspired.

You deserve it!

SKI

SWEET-ST E SCRU

BA

OATY ALOE BACK RUB

SM

DAZZLING-DUO ORGANI

N

MEGA-VEDA MASK

B[illegible]ISH-BUSTER FACIAL

ANA SPLIT BODY POLISH

OCEAN [illegible]ENCH

OOTHERS

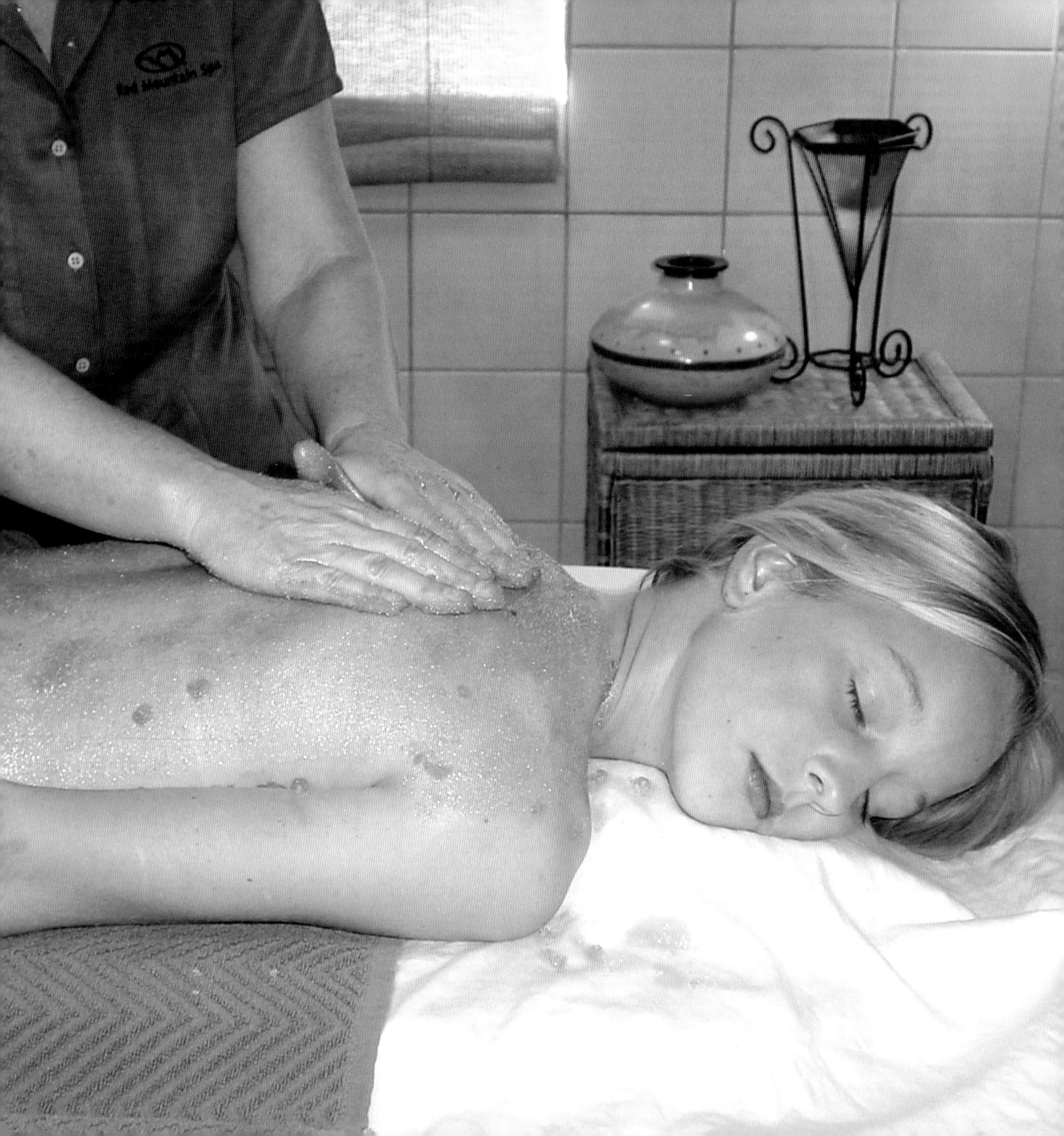

There's nothing more attractive than healthy, radiant skin. Treated right, your skin can be your most important beauty asset. Unfortunately, it can also be your worst nightmare. Few teens have perfect skin, and when your face freaks out, it's hard to feel good.

Most spas offer a whole menu of skin treatments, some to moisturize dry skin, others to zap zits or soothe blotchy areas. We've gathered the best of the best, so whatever your skin dilemma—too oily, too dry, too irritated—there's a treatment here for you! Deep-clean your way to a clear complexion with the Blemish-Buster Facial. Get glowing with the Sweet-Stuff Scrub. Turn up the heat with a Wrap-Me-Up Kelp Cocoon, or smooth flaky skin with the Banana Split Body Polish. Time to say buh-bye to confusing complexions. Take a tip from the pros and get skin savvy!

Red Mountain Spa

Dazzling-Duo Organic Facial

The word is out. Organic is in. Go au naturel with an organic facial that buffs and de-blemishes. This two-part treatment begins with a gentle scrub that sweeps away dullness and draws out oil, then seals the deal with a bacteria-banishing mask. A special mummy-inspired facial method is used to lock in moisture and soothe your skin.

inspiration

Organic Layer Cake Facial

OIL & WATER SKINCARE AND BROW DESIGN
SAN FRANCISCO, CA

At Oil & Water Skincare and Brow Design, all-organic ingredients are used in a relaxing plant, herb, and fruit-based facial. The plants contained in the products are rich in healing and soothing properties, and are grown without the use of any chemicals or pesticides.

In this special facial, organic masks and solutions are layered on top of each other, so each yummy product has more time to do its magic on the skin, giving it the very best nutrients it needs to stay healthy and feel fabulous. Some of the great natural treats include a foamy eucalyptus cleanser that removes surface impurities, followed by a wild plum toner, a rosehip and maize scrub, and a seven-herb treatment featuring ground ivy and dandelion to soothe and nourish the skin, minimizing redness. Finally, there's a leave-on mask blended for your skin type—sour cherry to tighten the pores, or carrot, honey, and vanilla to add extra moisture.

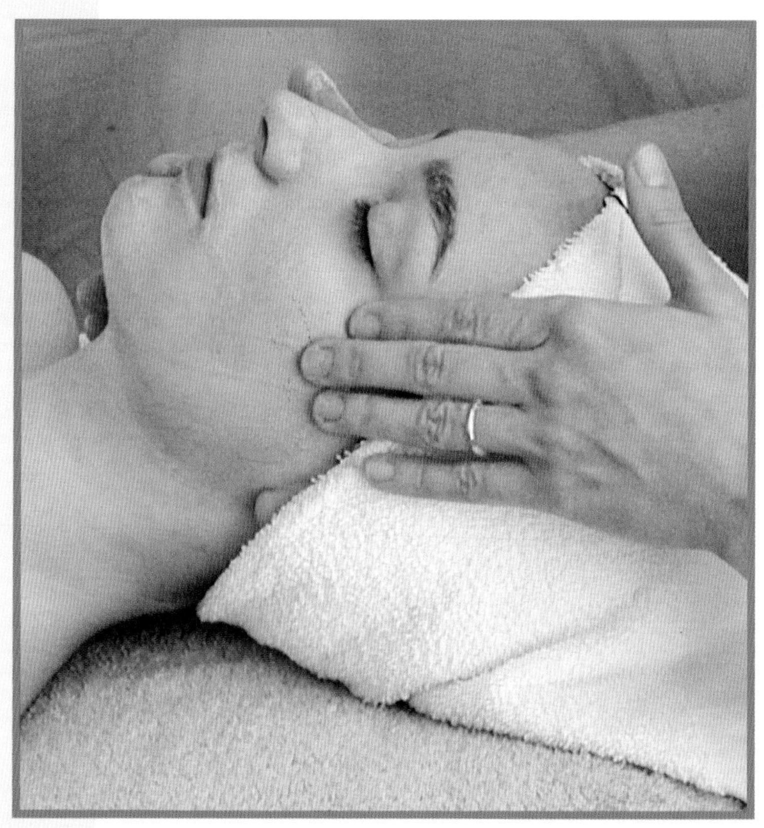

Oil & Water Skincare and Brow Design

✱ **Lemon fresh.** A natural exfoliant and antioxidant, citric acid is used in many cosmetics to brighten the skin and discourage bacteria. For a quick boost that helps control oil, apply a teaspoon of lemon juice to clean skin. Leave on for 5 minutes, then rinse well with warm water.

Here's How...

MUST HAVES

- 1 1/2 cups water
- 2 chamomile teabags
- 1/4 cup plain yogurt
- 1/4 cup honey
- squeeze of lemon juice
- 1/4 cup dry oatmeal (not the instant kind)
- unscented paper towels

STEP I

1. Boil 1 cup of the water and pour it into a wide bowl. Add the teabags and allow to steep for 10 minutes.
2. Pour the yogurt, honey, and lemon juice into another bowl, mixing thoroughly. Set aside.
3. In a third bowl, mix the oatmeal with 1/2 cup cool or lukewarm water.
4. Wash your face with a gentle cleanser and pat dry. Then use your fingers to gently massage the oatmeal mixture over your face, using a circular motion.
5. Leave the mixture on your skin for 5 minutes, then rinse off with warm water and pat dry.

STEP II

1. Smooth on an even layer of the honey-yogurt mask.
2. Dip 5 to 8 paper towels, one by one, into the tea. Wring gently, and place each one over a different area of your face to create the mummy effect. Leave your mouth and nostrils free so you can still breathe easily. (Hint: It helps if you're lying down, so the tissues stay in place.)
3. Relax for 15 minutes, then rinse your face again using cool water to seal in the moisture and close your pores against bacteria.

"Be hands-off. That means, don't touch your face! Breakouts can be minimized when you avoid picking or squeezing. Be aware of how often you touch your face, whether it's resting your chin in your hands or rubbing your face when you're tired. Wash your hands frequently, and clean off your phone to help with break-outs around the mouth."

—Lisa Tabbush, Oil & Water Skincare and Brow Design

✳ **Carrot cure.** If your skin has broken out, skip the oatmeal scrub and try this healing alternative: Finely grate one medium carrot in the blender, and smooth it over your skin. Rinse, and follow with the honey-yogurt mask. Carrots are rich in vitamin A, a powerful antiseptic that fights acne. Take that!

Sweet-Stuff Scrub

It's official. Sugar is good for you—or at least good for your skin. Take the sweet approach to restore your skin's natural radiance. This formula combines the moisturizing benefits of honey with the gentle exfoliation of sugar crystals. Add to that protein-rich egg yolks, and you've got a scrub that leaves your body healthy, nourished, and all aglow.

inspiration

Maple Sugar Body Scrub

TOPNOTCH RESORT AND SPA
STOWE, VT

Maple sugar has a great stimulating ability, revving up the circulatory system to restore a natural radiance to the skin. The Maple Sugar Body Scrub at Topnotch Resort and Spa taps into the benefits of the natural sugars of the New England maples that blanket the landscape.

This special treatment is intended to scrub away dry, dead skin cells, allowing the skin to renew itself faster. Crystallized granules of sugar are rubbed onto the back and legs and left to dissolve for a few minutes. At first, the pure maple granules are a little scratchy, but within minutes, when the granules dissolve, the skin begins to feel gloriously soft. For further exfoliation, the therapist uses a soft loofah mitt and massages the skin in flowing, circular motions with an oatmeal- and cornmeal-based soap that is made locally in small batches. A warm shower rinses off the excess sugar and other scrub particles. Maple sugar, oatmeal, cornmeal—the ingredients to a great breakfast, and to silky smooth skin.

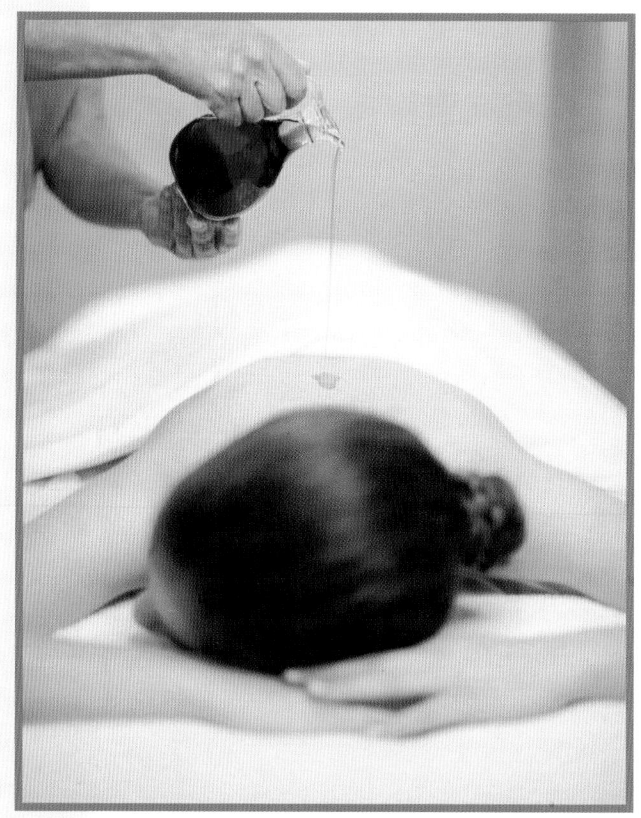

Topnotch Resort and Spa

✱ **Go nuts.** If your skin is especially dry, try substituting a tablespoon of ground almonds for the sugar. Almonds not only make a mean exfoliant, they're also rich in essential oils that nourish and moisturize the skin.

Here's How...

MUST HAVES

- 2 egg yolks
- 4 tablespoons honey
- 6 tablespoons olive or vegetable oil
- 1 tablespoon granulated white or brown sugar

1. Drop the egg yolks into a small bowl and stir lightly. Add honey and oil, mixing thoroughly.
2. Stir in the sugar and mix well. The goal is to achieve a nice slushy consistency, so add a little more oil or sugar as needed.
3. Get in the shower, and use a washcloth or loofah to massage the mixture onto wet skin. Rinse well with lukewarm water, then finish with a soothing moisturizer.

"The Maple Sugar Body Scrub is a unique exfoliating and softening body polishing that uses real maple sugar directly from Vermont's own maple trees. The treatment removes dead skin cells and replenishes lost moisture to the skin, for the ultimate hydrating experience."

—Alex Robinson, Topnotch Resort and Spa

✶ **Foil the oil.** If your skin is super-oily and prone to breakouts, cut the amount of olive oil in half or just leave it out altogether (you can add a little more honey to pump up the volume).

Sluff-Your-Stuff Hand & Foot Scrub

It's easy to forget about your skin in pursuit of some fun in the sun. But a little TLC can go a long way. Exfoliating, which basically means smoothing a gently abrasive cream on the skin and massaging the dead cells away, has an invigorating effect on the body, stimulating skin and getting the circulation going. This dryness-defying formula moisturizes nails and cuticles, while using the power of salt to turn rough hands and feet silky-soft.

inspiration

Back from the Beach Package

SPA AT THE DEL
HOTEL DEL CORONADO
CORONADO, CA

After surfing, kayaking, or soaking up the rays, treat your tired hands and feet to an exfoliation and massage. Scrubbing away layers of sand and suntan lotion after a day in the sun will leave your skin feeling soft, smooth, and tingly clean. The Back from the Beach Package at the Hotel del Coronado's Spa & Fitness Center combines sea salt with essential oils of lavender, citrus, or rosemary for a custom-made sea salt rub that is slathered all over the arms and lower legs. It leaves the skin glowing and brings sun-tired limbs back to life.

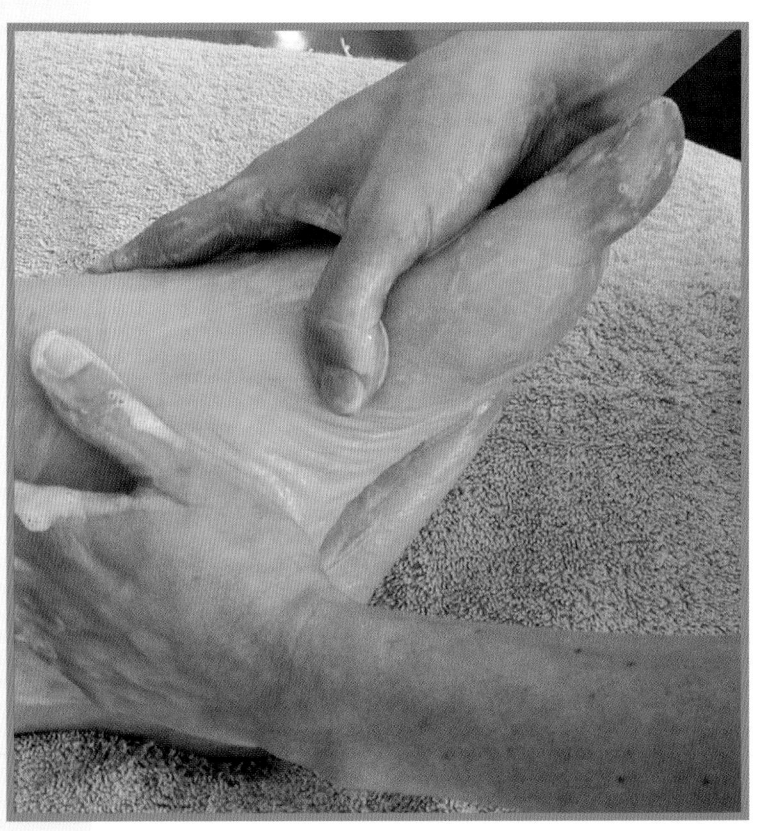

Spa at the Del

✳ **Bake-off.** Jennifer White, a Spa at the Del pro, recommends pampering your hands and feet at home with this super-moisturizing treatment: Soak your hands and feet in hot water with a few tablespoons of baking soda. After 30 minutes, dry off and apply your favorite moisturizer.

Here's How...

MUST HAVES

- 2 tablespoons olive or vegetable oil
- 2 tablespoons liquid hand soap
- 2 tablespoons kosher salt, table salt, or medium-coarse-grind sea salt

1. Pour the oil and liquid soap into a bowl, stirring them thoroughly. Stir in the salt, mixing well until evenly distributed.
2. Add a little water as needed, until the mixture is sudsy enough to lather.
3. Using a circular motion, massage the scrub into wet hands and feet. Spend extra time on calloused spots, the areas between your fingers and toes, and your nail beds and cuticles.
4. Let the scrub sit on your skin for about 5 minutes, then rinse well with lukewarm water.
5. Finish with a soothing moisturizer.

"A few precautions and a little common sense can fend off the ill-effects of sunlight and keep surfing, swimming, and all that stuff fun. Anyone who spends time in the sun needs to recognize the importance of using sunscreen lotions throughout the day—and taking good care of the skin afterwards."

—Jennifer White, Spa at the Del

✳ **Rub-a-double.** Whip up an extra batch for the shower, and use it with a loofah, sponge, or washcloth to create an all-over glow. (To keep the formula fresh for up to a week, store it in the fridge.)

✳ **Lemon aid.** Try adding 1 or 2 drops of lemon essential oil to the mix. This strengthens the nail bed, and adds a delicious, energy-boosting scent. Essential oils can be found at many pharmacies and at most health food stores.

Banana Split Body Polish

Fighting dry, flaky skin can be a full-time job, especially in the cold-weather months. This delicious banana rubdown, which is rich in potassium and vitamin A, will leave your skin soft and nourished. Plus, it smells as yummy as it sounds.

inspiration 

Tutti Frutti Scrub

THE PRIMA DONNA SPA FOR TEENS
ALLEGRIA SPA, PARK HYATT BEAVER CREEK
BEAVER CREEK, CO

In the heart of ski country, where frigid temperatures can leave skin dry and scaly, the Tutti Frutti Scrub at the Prima Donna Spa for Teens keeps wind-beaten skin smooth and glowing.

At the Tiki Scrub bar, teens concoct their own custom body scrub, using a base of sea salt, oatmeal, or brown sugar. Sea salt and brown sugar act as exfoliants, thanks to their granular texture, while oatmeal has a calming effect on the skin. The sea salt also helps draw out toxins, hydrate the skin, soothe sore muscles, and encourage cellular regeneration. To finish off their custom scrub, teens get a choice of the finest essential oils, including mango, chocolate chip, orange, sugar cookie, and more. The essential oils moisturize, regenerate, and nourish the skin, restoring its elasticity.

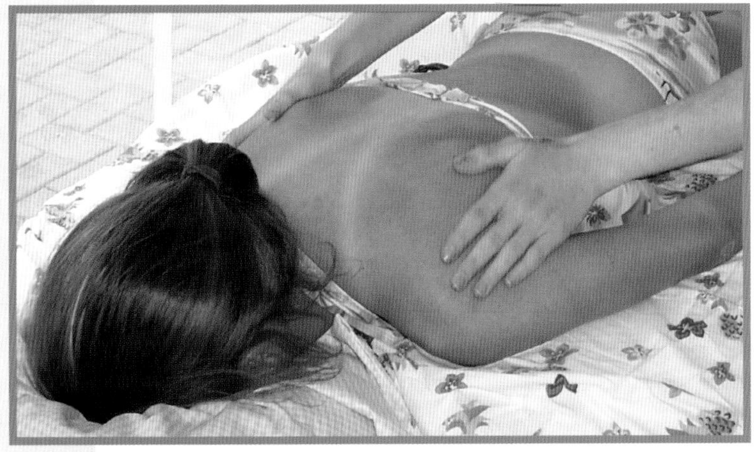

The Prima Donna Spa for Teens

* **Be nice.** Rubbing your skin too hard can cause redness and irritation. Let the scrub do all the work, and use slow, circular motions to gently exfoliate the skin and keep your body happy.

Here's How...

MUST HAVES

- 1 overripe banana
- 1/3 cup grape seed or canola oil (for drier skin), or 1/3 cup blend of honey and aloe gel (for oily or acne-prone skin)
- 2/3 cup brown sugar or medium-coarse-grind sea salt
- 1/2 teaspoon ground cinnamon (optional)

1. Place the banana in a bowl, and use a spoon to mash it up well.
2. Add the oil or honey and aloe mixture, mixing thoroughly to combine.
3. Add the sugar or salt, continuing to mash the mixture until it is slushy and even. Add cinnamon for extra spice.
4. Step into the shower, and use a bath brush, washcloth, or loofah to massage the scrub onto wet skin. Rinse well with lukewarm water, and finish with a soothing moisturizer.

"Before any exfoliating treatment, which can be a bit scratchy at first, make sure you are not sunburned, or the exfoliation will hurt. The rule of thumb is when skiing, and really every day, wear sunscreen: Sunscreen, sunscreen, sunscreen, is the mantra I give every teen who walks through these doors."

—Tiana Nixon, the Prima Donna Spa for Teens

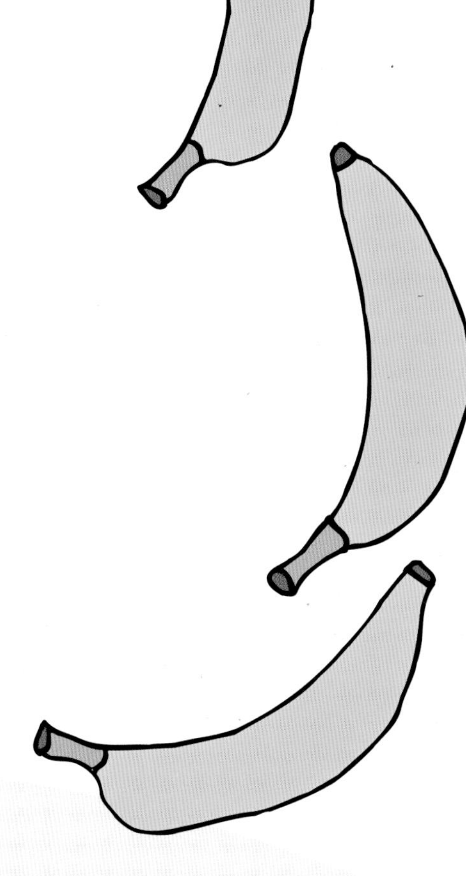

✶ **Tropical punch.** For an instant island getaway, try this heavenly twist: Substitute 1/2 cup chopped fresh pineapple for the bananas, and add 2 to 3 drops coconut oil in place of the cinnamon.

✶ **Skip the soap.** Take a lukewarm shower right after the scrub, and hide the soap bar until tomorrow. Sudsy water and excessive heat will break down all those moisturizing oils, and prevent them from soaking into your skin.

Oaty Aloe Back Scrub

It's time to watch your back. Literally! It may not be visible to the whole world all the time, but just like your chin, it can be prone to breakouts. So before your back makes its next public appearance, pamper it the same way you would your face. Buff your back with this super-exfoliating rubdown, and see why the aloe plant has been making the beauty charts for over 5,000 years. Despite its prickly surface, the aloe vera plant is filled with a rich hydrating ingredient that has a fresh fragrance and strong healing properties. Aloe gel is widely available, and pairs perfectly with almonds to slough off dirt and smooth you anew.

inspiration

Botanical Back Facial

THE SPA AT CAMELBACK INN
A JW MARRIOTT RESORT AND SPA
SCOTTSDALE, AZ

The Botanical Back Facial at the Spa at Camelback Inn is basically a facial with a back flip. To prepare for any skin treatment, the first step is always a thorough cleansing. Then the back steaming begins. Hot air is puffed onto the back to open up the pores and ready the skin for a deeper cleaning. To remove dead cells, a sugar scrub is rubbed on. Then a hydrating cactus mask is applied for a few minutes, and removed with hot towels. For maximum relaxation, the grand finale is a 10-minute back, leg, foot, and scalp massage.

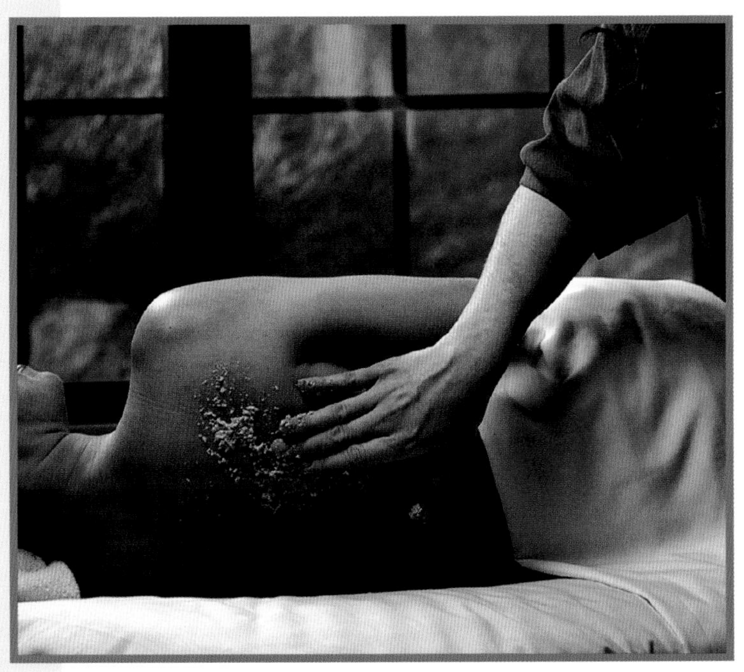

The Spa at Camelback Inn

* **Beach blitz.** If your heart belongs to the sand and surf, even full-throttle SPF doesn't always cut it. When the sun's rays leave you toasted, this quick aloe cure-all will soothe the burn and help prevent peeling: Mix 1/2 cup aloe gel with 1 teaspoon chamomile tea. Smooth on the affected area a few times a day until healed.

Here's How...

1. Combine all ingredients in a bowl and stir until well mixed.
2. Step into the shower, and wash and rinse your body. Use your fingers to apply the formula to as much of your back and shoulders as you can reach. (Hint: ask a friend for help in covering those to hard-to-reach spots.) Leave on the skin for 10 minutes.
3. Use a gentle circular motion to slough your skin with the brush, washcloth, or loofah. (If your back is very broken out, skip this step and just rinse thoroughly to avoid irritating the skin.)
4. Rinse well with warm water, and pat excess moisture from the skin. Follow with a soothing mix of aloe gel and your favorite moisturizer.

MUST HAVES

- 2/3 cup aloe vera gel
- 1 cup finely ground oats (not instant—too mushy)
- 2 tablespoons finely ground almonds
- 4 teaspoons honey
- long-handled brush, washcloth, or loofah

"One of the most neglected parts of the body is the back, so it is important to do proper back cleansing. Get a loofah scrub with a long handle, and make sure to cleanse the back every time you take a shower. There are also a lot of spritzer products that can be easily applied to the back to help fight bacteria and hydrate."

—Gloria Szekely-Rogue, The Spa at Camelback Inn

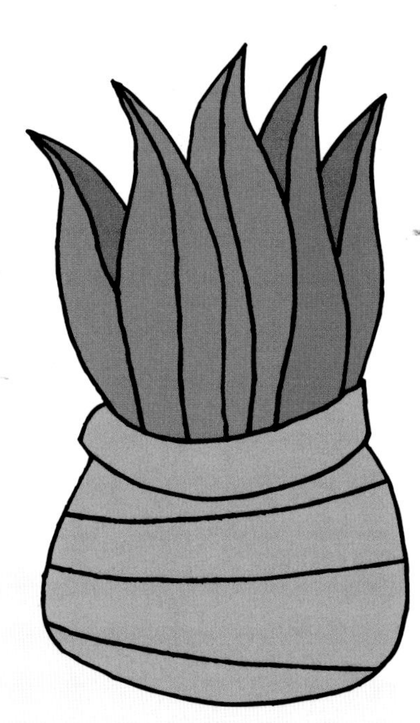

✳ **Lip saver.** Like the back, lips often get overlooked until they're in need of rescue. Keep them kissable with a moisture-rich lip gloss that soothes and heals: Combine 1/2 teaspoon of aloe gel with 1/2 teaspoon of petroleum jelly, and store in a small plastic tub (available at many pharmacies and beauty supply stores).

Mega-Veda Mask

Tap into the ancient wisdom of Ayurveda to give your skin the stuff it craves. Ayurveda is an ancient Indian philosophy that places people into three different "Doshas," or body categories. For each Dosha there are specific guidelines to balance body, mind, and spirit. To mix up the perfect mask, use our quick guide to determine your Dosha. Then raid the kitchen for the fruits, vegetables, and other organic ingredients ideal for your skin type.

inspiration

Ayurvedic Facial

THE SPA AT THE BROADMOOR
COLORADO SPRINGS, CO

At the Spa at the Broadmoor, clients begin by filling out a questionnaire on their body and skin type, eating preferences, and general habits to determine their dominant Dosha. They are then pampered with a facial that is customized accordingly.

If you have dry Vata skin, technicians will use a rich, nourishing cleanser, with ingredients like oatmeal, almond meal, and cream, that won't strip natural oils from your skin. If your predominant Dosha is Pitta, and you have sensitive skin, a gentle herbal cleanser will purify without irritating. Sandalwood in fine oatmeal with a little cooling milk and rosewater makes a gentle Pitta-pacifying cleanser. For oily Kapha types, a stimulating product that contains oil-balancing herbs like lavender helps to cleanse and clarify the skin.

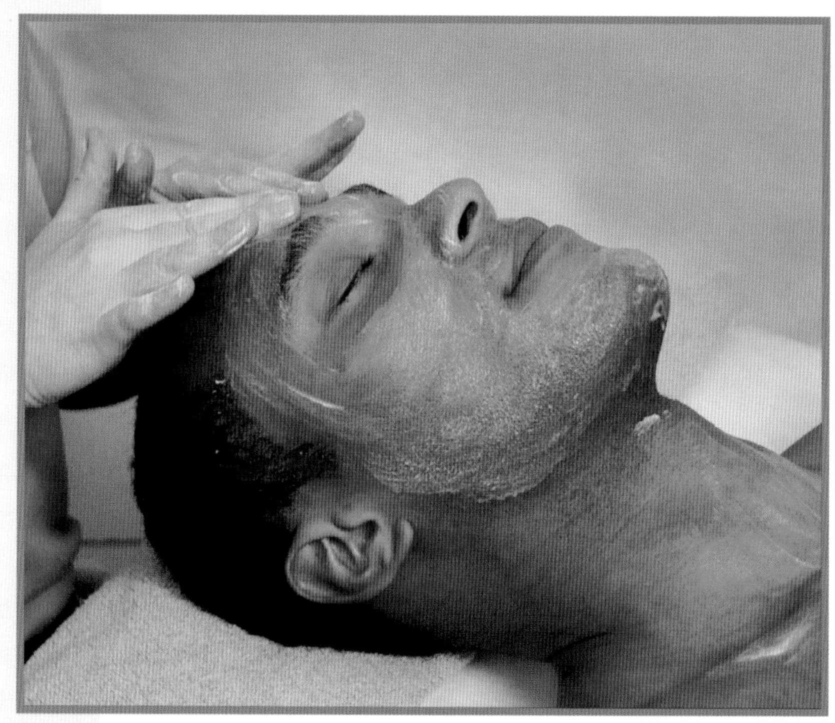

The Spa at the Broadmoor

The choices you make at mealtime have serious impact on your skin. Follow these Dosha-tips to get glowing from the inside out.

What's Your Dosha?

Vata Vata skin tends to be dry and flaky, especially in winter. Vatas need plenty of nourishment and hydration to counteract dryness and the effects of the environment. Rich, hydrating ingredients give your skin the moisture it needs.

VATA MUST HAVES

- 1/2 carrot, grated
- 1 avocado, mashed
- 2 tablespoons almond or sesame oil

Pitta Extra-sensitive Pitta is also known as "combination skin": oily in the T-zone (forehead, nose, and chin), and dry in other areas. Pittas break out easily under stress, so you'll get the most from a mask with mild, creamy ingredients that calm and soothe.

PITTA MUST HAVES

- 1 overripe banana, mashed
- 1/2 small cucumber, grated
- 2 tablespoons coconut milk or plain whole-milk yogurt

Kapha Kapha skin is extra-oily, with a tendency toward acne and enlarged pores. Highly acidic fruits and other oil-reducing ingredients are your best bet for keeping shine, blackheads, and breakouts at bay.

KAPHA MUST HAVES

- 1 medium apple, grated (green ones are best)
- 1 egg white
- 2 tablespoons lemon juice

Here's How...

1. Wash your face with a gentle cleanser and pat dry.
2. Place all your ingredients in a bowl, mixing thoroughly to combine.
3. Use your fingers to apply a thin, even layer of the mask over your face, avoiding the eye area.
4. Kick back with a book or meditate for 20 minutes.
5. Use a washcloth and tepid water to rinse off the mask. Pat dry.

"Doshas relate to the entire body: The skin, the body's largest organ, is the first place to show signs of any internal imbalances. When the body is balanced, the skin's appearance will be clear, radiant, and exude a healthy glow. When there is an internal imbalance—stress, disease, unruliness—the skin shows blemishes, ruddiness, and uneven tone."

—Naoma Ford, The Spa at the Broadmoor

✶ **Vata.** When you're looking for a snack, go for rich, dense foods like milk, oats, bananas, almonds, and sunflower seeds.

✶ **Pitta.** Stick to less spicy foods to keep your skin balanced. Apples, avocado, watermelon, lettuce, and chickpeas are all on your menu.

✶ **Kapha**. Reach for lighter foods to combat the oil. Apricots, peaches, broccoli, tomatoes, chicken, and fish are all good ways to go.

Ocean Drench

Seawater and products of the sea have long been prized for their nutrient-rich content and natural healing properties. Seaweed and sea salt are both packed with nutrients that work to detoxify and revitalize your body. Once you've experienced the amazing effects of seawater, you'll understand why so many spas spring up by the beach. Here's how to skip the trip seaside and turn your tub into a private ocean retreat.

inspiration

Tub, Scrub, and Rub

SEA WATER SPA AT GURNEY'S INN
MONTAUK, NY

At the Sea Water Spa at Gurney's Inn, "rub-a-dub-dub" takes on a whole new meaning with the Tub, Scrub, and Rub treatment. This is no ordinary bath—Gurney's Inn is currently the only true Thalasso spa in the United States.

"Thalasso" is the Greek word for sea. Seawater from the Atlantic Ocean is pumped directly into the tubs, Roman baths, and pool. Participants are first exfoliated with a seaweed toning gel. Then the bath begins: 94 degrees is the optimum water temperature for the absorption of the nutrients and minerals in the seawater. Blasts of soothing seawater from the jets in the tub relax muscles, and tone the skin. The combination of seawater and jets makes this bath unique. After the tub, there's the "rub"—a luxurious Swedish body massage.

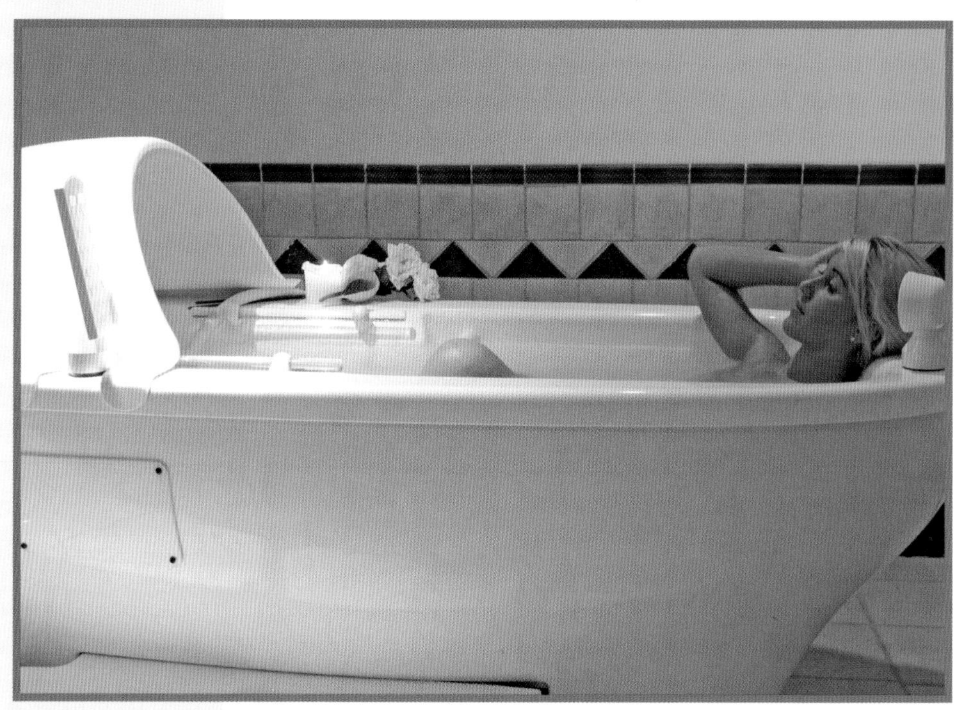

Sea Water Spa at Gurney's Inn

✳ **Beach baby.** To turn your bathroom into a sea retreat, run with the marine theme: Light fragrant candles, drop in marine-scented bath beads, and use a seashell as a salt scoop.

Here's How...

MUST HAVES

- 1/2 pound sea salt
- 1 1/2 pounds baking soda
- 3 teaspoons kelp seaweed powder (available at health food stores and online herbal outlets)
- essential oil of rosemary or lavender (optional)

1. Fill the tub high enough so that the water will cover you when you're lying down. You'll want the water to be warm but not super-hot—anywhere between 90 and 100 degrees is ideal for releasing impurities and absorbing nutrients. (Use a thermometer if you need to.)
2. Pour in the salt, baking soda, and kelp powder. Boost the bath's soothing effect by adding a few drops of essential oil.
3. Soak in the tub until the water has cooled, around 20 minutes. You marine mammal, you.

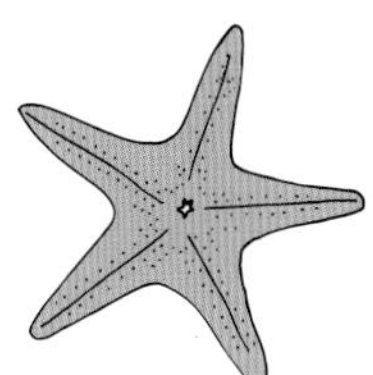

"Head for the sea whenever you can. The sea has been our healer since the beginning of time. Seawater contains 120 chemical elements in the form of salts and dissolved gas. The skin absorbs magnesium, calcium, sodium, iodine, silicon, zinc, selenium, sulfur, and fluoride, all in the proper combinations present in nature. Even beach-walking at the edge of the sea promotes the inhalation of the minerals, which are then absorbed by the capillaries directly into the bloodstream."

—Susan Yunker, Sea Water Spa at Gurney's Inn

✳ **Mineral city.** Sea salt is full of detoxifying minerals like calcium and iron. If you can get Dead Sea salt, it is even more intense: When you bathe with it, you don't even need to use soap—the minerals cleanse the skin all on their own.

Blemish-Buster Facial

If your acne-prone skin has you hiding from the world, help is on the way. Demolish breakouts, and keep new ones at bay, with this fruity, blemish-fighting facial. It applies three power principles—deep-cleansing, detoxifying, and toning. The honey is great for eliminating bacteria, while strawberries contain salicylic acid, a key acne-fighting agent. Learn how to scrub, moisturize, and keep your skin clear with this basic acne-busting facial.

inspiration

Teen Acne Buster Facial

TIFFANI KIM INSTITUTE
CHICAGO, IL

At the Tiffani Kim Institute, top skin-care gurus solve challenging acne problems once and for all. The Teen Acne Buster Facial is all about saving face—not only treating visible pimples, but getting to the build-up forming under the skin to help shut down the acne cycle.

Tiffani Kim skin experts call themselves "acne busters" and believe facials are the best preventative medicine for blemishes. By cleansing, toning, and exfoliating the skin, they remove dead skin cells that can clog the pores and cause acne. Skin technicians also get at the root of the problem by asking lifestyle questions—could the line of pimples across your forehead be caused by that grungy baseball cap, or the bangs on your forehead? Teens are given customized step-by-step instructions on everything they need to keep their skin clear and clean.

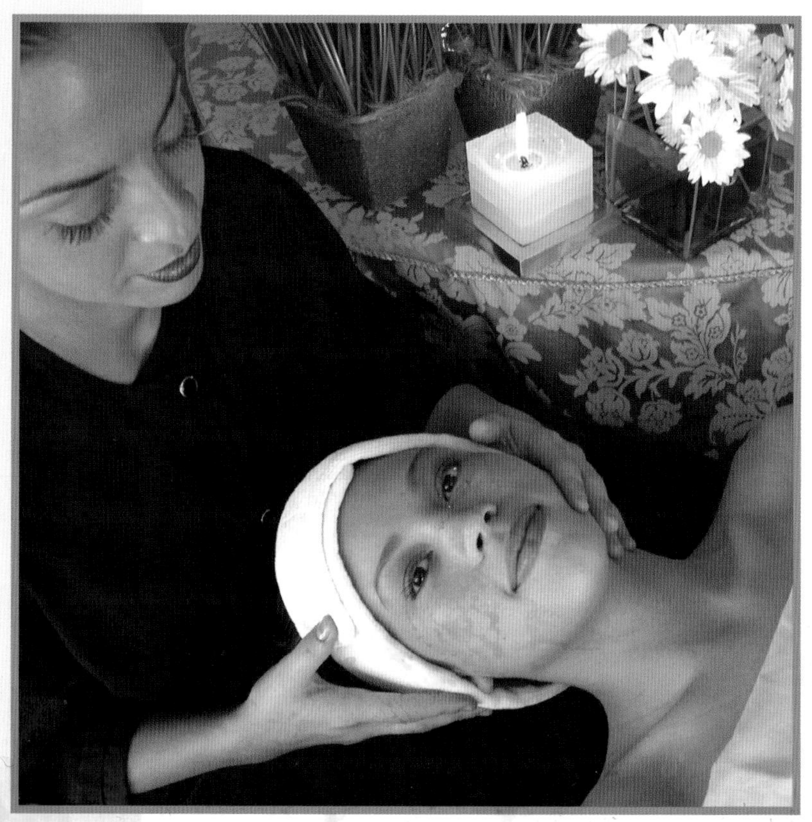

Tiffani Kim Institute

* **Call a truce.** When breakouts occur, resist the urge to declare war on your face. Picking and squeezing can turn a tiny spot into an angry flare-up that takes days to heal. Be gentle and keep your hands away—your skin will thank you.

Here's How...

MUST HAVES

- 1/2 cup strawberries
- 2 teaspoons honey
- 1 egg white
- 2 cucumber slices
- 3 peppermint teabags
- 3 washcloths
- moisturizer

1. Mash the strawberries in a bowl, using the back of a spoon. Add the honey and egg white, mixing thoroughly until smooth.

2. Wash your face with a gentle cleanser and pat dry. Use your fingers to apply a thin, even layer of the strawberry mask all over your face, except around your eyes. Lie back, throw those cucumber slices over your lids, and rest for 15 to 20 minutes. (Hint: Stress is a huge factor in causing breakouts. Take this time to slow down, and just breathe.) Rinse off the mask with tepid water and pat dry.

3. Fill the sink or a large bowl with hot water, and add the teabags. Throw a towel over your head to create a tent, and bend over the water for 10 to 15 minutes to let the steam open your pores. Peppermint is not only invigorating, it's especially good for healing blemishes.

4. Rinse your face well, then dip a washcloth in cool water. Wring, and place it over your face. This closes the pores, so the acne-causing bacteria can't sneak back in.

5. Apply a light, oil-free moisturizer.

"You can eat your way to good skin. Eat tons of fresh salmon, kiwi, avocado, eggs, and spinach. These foods attract water to your cells, and give you a radiant glow."

—Catrinceer Carter, Tiffani Kim Institute

✳ **Moisture myth.** Teens with oily skin tend to skip the moisturizer and use harsh products that strip and over-dry. Problem is, this kicks the oil glands into high gear to compensate, which leads to even more breakouts. Apply a non-comedogenic (non-acne-causing) moisturizer every day, and use a gentle, non-stripping toner to keep your skin balanced and hydrated.

Wrap-Me-Up Kelp Cocoon

Turn up the heat with a detox concoction that makes you feel smooth and glowing all over. This hydrating body treat revives dull skin and sends impurities packing (try it the day before you hit the beach!). Grab a friend to help you create the cocoon, and then get ready to look radiant.

inspiration 

Dead Sea and Chamomile Mud Wrap

SEVENTEEN STUDIO SPA SALON
PLANO, TX

At Seventeen Studio Spa Salon, mud takes on a life of its own in a deep-cleansing specialty treatment that gently exfoliates and detoxifies the skin.

The Dead Sea and Chamomile Mud Wrap draws its benefits from the brownish clay mud collected from the mineral-rich Dead Sea. Slivers of mineralized seaweed and essential oils, including lavender, chamomile, and marigold, are added to the mud, and help to remove dull skin cells and add moisture for softer and smoother skin. The one-hour treatment begins with an exfoliation, to get rid of any dry skin cells. The mud is then slathered on the body from neck to feet, and warm blankets are wrapped around the body to seal in the benefits. After a shower, a light full-body massage with avocado and carrot oils further hydrates the skin.

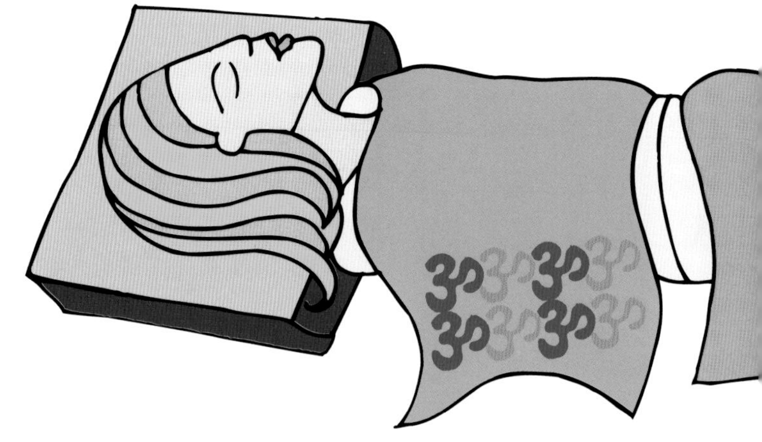

✳ **Extra mayo.** If your skin's especially dry, substitute 1/2 cup mayonnaise for the aloe gel to create a super-hydrating drench that leaves you velvety soft.

Here's How...

MUST HAVES

- 1 large avocado, mashed
- 1/4 cup kelp seaweed powder (available at natural food stores)
- 1/4 cup sea salt
- 1/2 cup aloe vera gel
- 1/4 cup water
- plastic drop cloth (available at hardware stores)
- medium-sized paintbrush (optional)
- large cotton sheet or two large towels (use ones you don't mind getting messy)

Note: The above materials serve one, so double them if you're taking turns!

1. Place the avocado, kelp powder, salt, and aloe gel in a bowl, and stir to combine. Then add just as much water as you need to create a pasty mud.
2. Spread out the drop cloth on your bed or the floor.
3. Toss the towels in the dryer for 10 minutes on high heat.
4. Use the paintbrush or your fingers to slather the mixture all over your body.
5. Lie down on the drop cloth and have your friend wrap it around you like a cocoon. Then have her cover you up with the hot towels.
6. Relax and enjoy the toasty warmth for 10 minutes. (Hint: This treatment works by purifying your pores. The more you sweat, the better!)

"The mud treatment does more than just detox and smooth the skin, it really helps remove all the toxins in the body. You immediately notice a feeling of being more energized and feeling better all over."

—Tamela Shafer, Seventeen Studio Spa Salon

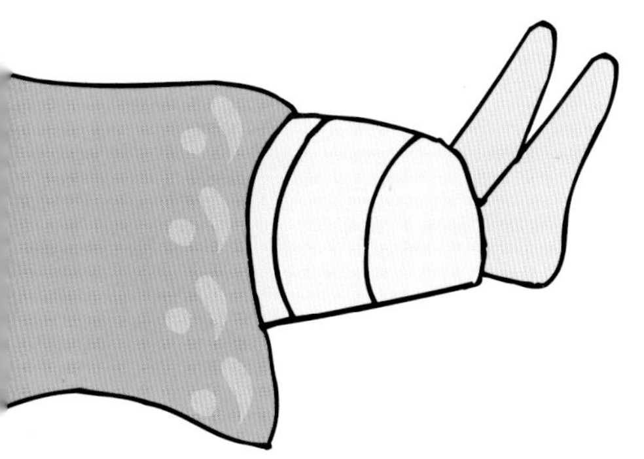

✷ **Add a 'nana.** For extra-oily skin that's prone to breakouts, the fatty acids in avocado can send oil glands into overdrive. Skip the risk while re-creating the nourishing effects of mud by using a potassium-rich banana instead.

BO

RED ROCK LET WRA

SELF-SOO MAS E

ALOHA GROOVES

BU

HOME STRETC

DY

OUT WN

P TUR PERFECT PLIE

KICK-START ALPINE MUESLI

ILDERS

Are you too tired for tennis? Too beat for basketball? Too bored to be bothered? If so, it may be time for a total body tune-up. One of the best ways to boost energy and build a strong, beautiful body is to take an active approach to living.

At the nation's top teen spas, cool workouts and workshops make getting healthy anything but dull. Whether you're a jock or a couch potato, we've found something to spark your curiosity and get you going. Indulge your inner island girl with an Aloha Grooves hula workout. Plié your way to perfect posture, then tone your abs with the Workout Rundown. Kick-start your morning with some yummy homemade muesli or refuel with a late-afternoon lettuce wrap. A healthy lifestyle has never felt—or tasted—so good!

The Spa at Norwich Inn

Workout Rundown

Personal trainers are a luxury, but you don't need one to get—and stay—fit. When you discover the exercise potential in everyday activities, it becomes easier than ever to take a rain-or-shine approach to working out. For best results, try to squeeze in 30 minutes of aerobic exercise at least three days per week.

inspiration

Teen Tune-Up

TOPNOTCH RESORT AND SPA
STOWE, VT

Ever wonder if you're getting the most out of your workout, achieving what you want in sports, or eating right? Teens get the lowdown on strength training, cardio, healthy eats, dieting, and more with the Teen Tune-Up at Topnotch Resort and Spa.

At Topnotch, the routine is one-on-one training. Personal trainers create 50-minute workouts which can include a series of drills, from body-sculpting exercises to calorie-torching cardio maneuvers. Depending on what each person wants to achieve, from strength training to weight loss or ski conditioning, trainers set up a routine targeted to individual goals. For a sculpted body, lifting lighter weights or more repetitions may be called for. To increase endurance, sprinting and long-distance running can do the trick. Teens walk away with a routine tailored to their needs, to work on either at home or at the gym.

Topnotch Resort and Spa

* **Make a date.** Some people hit their energy peak first thing in the morning; others can muster more intensity after school. Either way, choose a time and stick with it to keep yourself in the exercise groove.

Here's How...
Top 20 cardio-worthy ways to get fit

10 ways to fabulous fitness without leaving home

Activity	Calories burned in 30 minutes*
Jumping rope	300–350
Shoveling snow	250–300
Mowing the lawn (manual mower)	250–300
Walking up stairs	200–250
Gardening	250–300
Playing with the dog in the yard	150–200
Raking leaves	100–150
Vacuuming/mopping	75–125
Washing the car	75–125
Dusting	60–110

*estimates based on the average 120-pound person

10 ways to exercise (and socialize) on a sunny day

Activity	Calories burned in 30 minutes*
Mountain biking	300–400
Hiking	250–350
Playing tennis	200–250
Shooting baskets	200–250
Playing soccer	200–250
Playing softball	100–150
Playing volleyball	75–125
Playing ping-pong	60–110
Playing frisbee	60–110
Bowling	50–75

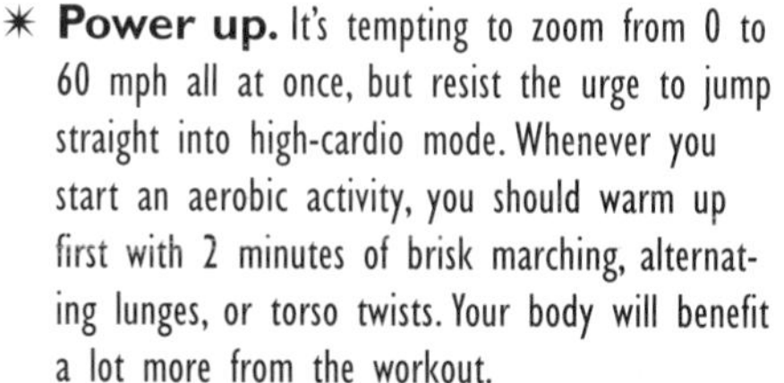

✳ **Power up.** It's tempting to zoom from 0 to 60 mph all at once, but resist the urge to jump straight into high-cardio mode. Whenever you start an aerobic activity, you should warm up first with 2 minutes of brisk marching, alternating lunges, or torso twists. Your body will benefit a lot more from the workout.

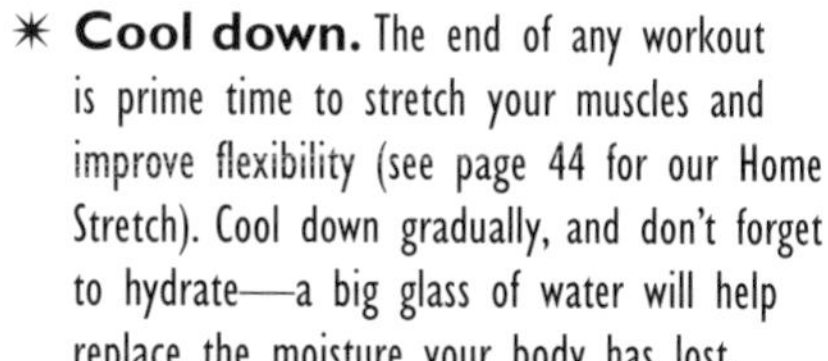

✳ **Cool down.** The end of any workout is prime time to stretch your muscles and improve flexibility (see page 44 for our Home Stretch). Cool down gradually, and don't forget to hydrate—a big glass of water will help replace the moisture your body has lost.

Aloha Grooves

Many people think crunches are the only abdominal exercise. But, believe it or not, hula dancing may be their new rival. Get the island vibe going with this tropical home workout. These basic steps are the foundation of all hula dancing—once you've got them down, you'll be ready to sway with the best of them. (Grass skirts and coconut shells optional.)

inspiration

Hip, Hop Hula

IHILANI SPA
JW MARRIOTT IHILANI RESORT AND SPA AT KO OLINA
KO OLINA, HI

At the Ihilani Spa, the traditional Hawaiian dance takes on a cool new twist with Hip, Hop Hula—a no-fuss fitness routine that gives you a great total body workout. Teens head out under the palm trees, plant their bare feet in the sand, and are tutored by a native Hawaiian "Kumu"—or "one with great respect and expertise." The hula is considered the language of the heart by the Hawaiian people, who interpret the lyrics of their lilting songs with graceful, swaying dance movements. After a warm-up, students learn basic hula movements that are later incorporated into more complex dances. But be warned: It's a lot trickier than it looks. Novice dancers can expect many falls into the sand and lots of laughter as they get into the swing of things.

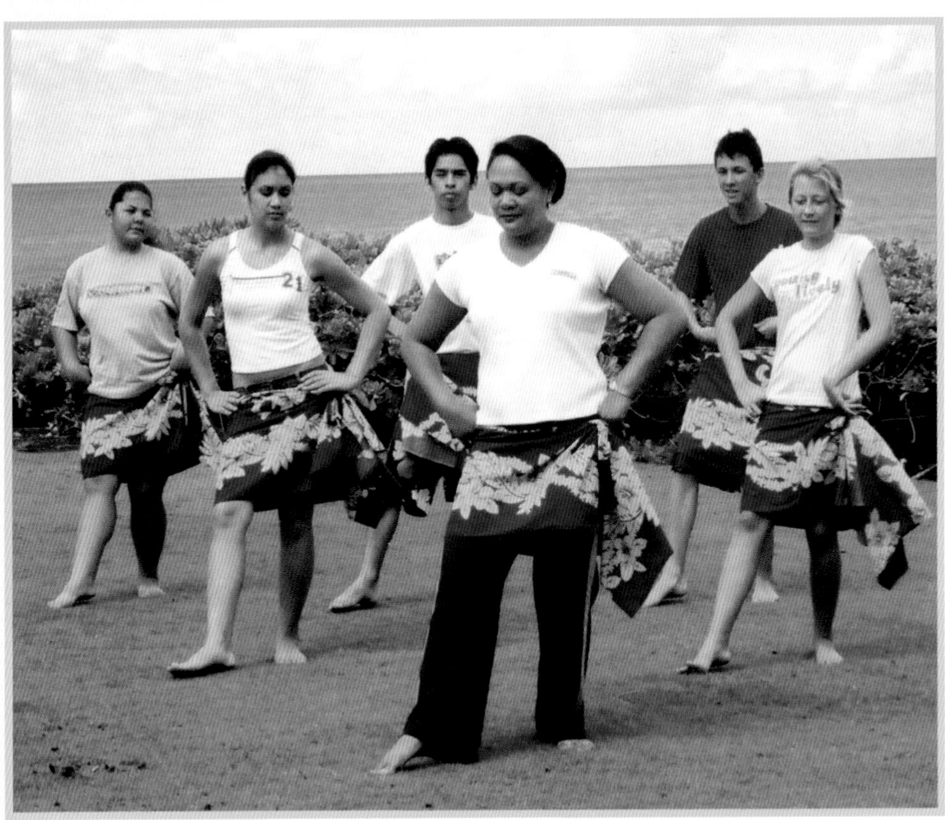

JW Marriott Ihilani Resort and Spa at Ko Olina

✳ **Tropical translation.** Though most people think of it as a greeting, the Hawaiian "aloha" has many meanings, including kindness, harmony, patience, and humility. For many Hawaiians and mainlanders, the aloha spirit is a way of life that's based on living consciously, joyously, and in the present.

Here's How...

Try incorporating 5–10 minutes of hula dancing into your fitness routine to strengthen your thighs, hips, and lower abs.

Kaholo (Traveling in Motion)

1. Stand with your feet in hula position (that is, right below your shoulders). Bend your knees slightly, and place your hands on your hips. Flatten your abs and keep them tight by pulling your belly button in toward your spine.

2. Now slide to the right, using this three-part step:

3. Push your hips out slightly to the left, then take a step to the right with your right foot.

4. Sway your hips from the left to the right and finish with a step to the right with your left foot (this last step is held a little longer).

5. Swing your hips back to the left and repeat the process above.

6. Now repeat the sequence on the other side. Push your hips out slightly to the right, then take a step to the left with your left foot.

7. Sway your hips from the right to the left, and finish with a step to the left with your right foot.

8. Swing your hips back to the right and repeat.

MUST HAVES

- medium-paced music—preferably something tropical
- comfortable clothes

Once you get in the groove, add the arm movements:

1. As you move to the right, extend your right arm out to the right side of your body, and cross your left arm over your chest, so it's pointing in the same direction.

2. As you sway to the left, switch to the other side. Your arms should be extended in the direction you're moving.

"We hope teens take home with them a little piece of the Hawaiian culture through the hula sessions. For centuries, Hawaiians had no written language and passed their history and story on through dance. It was a way for people to create their own stories. We encourage the teens to see it as a great way to express their uniqueness."

—Janette Goodman, JW Marriott Ihilani Resort and Spa at Ko Olina

✶ **Spirit style.** Even if you've never left the mainland, decorating your room with tropical touches can help get you in the aloha spirit. Floral prints, bright colors, and elements of nature are more than just stylish—their energizing colors and natural textures can help stimulate your mind and lift your mood.

Kick-Start Alpine Muesli

If your morning rush doesn't include a power-packed breakfast, it's time to revise your routine. A good breakfast not only kick-starts your brain, it also revs up your metabolism for the day. This Canyon Ranch recipe is the perfect combo of fruit, protein, and whole grains to give your day a delicious and healthy start.

inspiration

Nutritional Intelligence

CANYON RANCH
TUCSON, AZ AND LENOX, MA

At Canyon Ranch, nutritionists meet with teens one-on-one to discuss their individual concerns and decide together how to reach realistic individual health goals. During a minimum three-night stay, teens are coached on everything from snacking right to cooking light.

The program at Canyon Ranch is about helping people create habits they can stick with. Health professionals want to ensure that getting healthy is so much fun, teens will want to continue what they learn when they return home. Some general tips everyone can benefit from include starting the day with a hearty, nutrition-packed breakfast, snacking on healthy foods like nuts, fruits, and yogurts that contain natural sugars, and moderating coffee and chocolate. These simple tips help keep energy constant, and lessen the highs and lows that come from sudden bursts of caffeine and refined sugar. Whether you're interested in boosting athletic performance or just in eating better for overall health, the tools you learn from these professionals will start you on a course you can stay on for life.

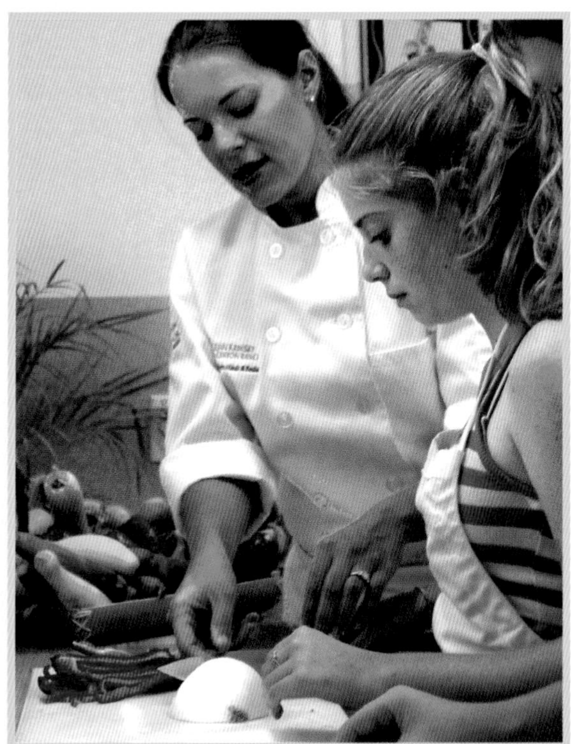

Krinsky/Canyon Ranch Young Adult Summer Program

✴ **Freeze fruit.** The beauty of buying frozen fruit is that it is picked ripe and available year-round, so you don't need to wait for your favorites to be in season. You can also make your own frozen fruit treats at home: Try a frozen banana mixed with yogurt for a creamy, irresistible dessert.

Here's How...

1. In a large bowl, combine the oatmeal, milk, yogurt, and vanilla. Let the mixture sit for 5 minutes to soften the oats.

2. In a small bowl, combine the orange juice, chopped nuts, and honey. Add the chopped apple and remaining fruit.

3. Stir the juice mixture into the yogurt mixture, and mix well. Serve chilled.

Makes 4 servings, each with about 290 calories and 10 grams of fat.

MUST HAVES

- 1/3 cup uncooked instant oatmeal
- 1/3 cup 2-percent milk
- 1/3 cup nonfat plain yogurt
- 1 teaspoon pure vanilla extract
- 1/2 cup orange juice
- 1/3 cup chopped almonds
- 2 tablespoons honey
- 2/3 cup peeled red apples, finely chopped
- 1 1/2 cups finely chopped mixed fresh fruit, such as peaches, pears, and strawberries

"One thing we stress most here is 'Don't diet!' We want to teach good eating habits that give teens the tools they need to keep their bodies healthy for life. We try to show them that it is not difficult, and, in fact, extremely fun to lead a healthy life."

—Jennifer Flora, Canyon Ranch

✳ **Take it to go.** Even if you don't have time to eat at home, skip the high-sugar "breakfast bars" and take a healthy homemade meal to go. Reusable plastic containers from the grocery store let you pack a serving of Kick-Start Alpine Muesli (or fruit and cheese, or yogurt and granola) the night before, so it's ready when you are.

Work-It Workout

Time to give your muscles a push! Strengthen and sculpt your body at home using nothing more than soup cans, a few pillows, and gravity. Start out by doing this routine twice a week, then bump it up to three times a week as you get stronger. Stick with it, and you'll start seeing results in six to eight weeks.

inspiration

Muscle Jam

ARIA SPA & CLUB
VAIL CASCADE RESORT & SPA
VAIL, CO

Fast-paced and action-packed, the Muscle Jam class at Aria Spa & Club turns teens on to the FIT work-out formula—Frequency, Intensity, and Time. Boosting your muscle strength will increase your metabolism, and make your body perform better at other activities. Pumping up your workout to the next level can also yield a host of benefits—in strength, stability, mobility, flexibility, and posture—not to mention the energy boost.

Aria Spa & Club

"Exercise with intensity and logic," says Dan Timm, Fitness Director at Aria, who encourages teens to push themselves harder, more intensely, more frequently, and longer. The no-fuss fitness class includes push-ups to build upper body and arm strength, a challenging jump-rope workout to build endurance and stronger leg muscles, and weight training. Abdominal crunches are also included to strengthen the core body. Teens who tough out the Muscle Jam formula are at less risk of injury, and gain a boost in self-esteem from testing their athletic limits to the max.

* **Don't push it.** Avoid muscle strain by listening to your body. If something hurts, stop. If you push too hard too soon, you risk fatigue, excessive soreness, or injury. Build up gradually, and leave at least one day between workouts to give your body a chance to recover.

Here's How...

MUST HAVES

- 2 15-ounce cans of soup
- 2 standard-size pillows
- high-intensity workout music
- comfortable clothes and workout shoes

There's a reason why these moves are legendary in the workout world: They're all easy to do and amazingly effective. Kick off your new routine with 8 repetitions of each exercise below (we guarantee you'll feel the burn). As the weeks pass, work your way up to 16 reps each.

SUPER SQUAT. This works the back of the thigh (hamstrings), the front of the thigh (quadriceps), and the buns (gluteus maximus).

1. Stand against a wall with your feet about hip-distance apart. Flex your abs, straighten your back, lift your chest, and stand tall.
2. Bend your knees, and pretend you're lowering yourself into a chair behind you. Keeping your back against the wall, sit down as far as you can while keeping your upper body as straight as possible. Don't overextend your knees—the goal is to get your thighs parallel to the floor. Straighten your legs, and stand back up.

TRICEPS TRYOUT. Tones the shoulders (deltoids), stomach (abdominals), and arms (biceps and triceps).

1. Lie down on the floor with your knees bent, feet flat on the floor. Grab a soup can in each hand. Raise your arms so they're pointing straight upward over your chest.
2. Lower the cans slowly behind you, until the bottom of each can is level with the back of your head. Straighten your arms. Flex your abs so your lower back doesn't arch.

✶ **Sock it to me.** As you get stronger, use other items from around the house to add more resistance to your workout. For homemade weights, fill two thick, doubled-up socks with pennies, and tie off the ends (use a kitchen scale to make sure they're the same weight).

PROPER PUSH-UP. Tones the chest (pectorals), shoulders (deltoids), and arms (biceps and triceps).

1. Lie on your stomach with your toes bent on the floor. Place your palms on the floor, a little wider than shoulder-distance apart. Straighten your arms and lift your body, balancing your weight between your palms and toes. Squeeze your abs and try to lift yourself up in a straight line so your back doesn't arch.
2. As you reach the top, begin to bend your arms again (don't lock your elbows). Use the strength of your arms and chest to lower your entire body in a straight line. When your upper arms are parallel to the floor, raise yourself up again.

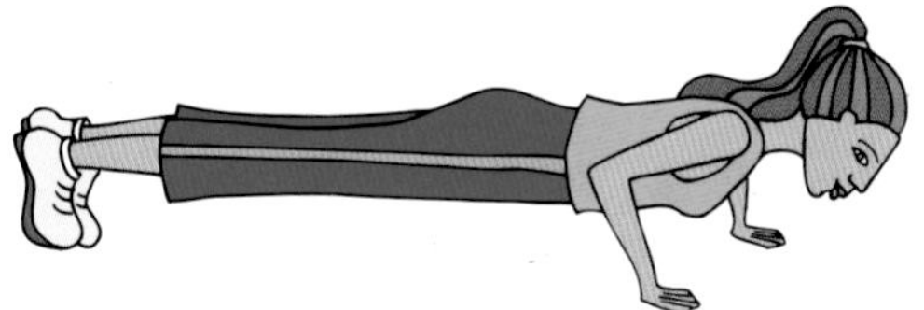

"Everyone is more motivated to work out if they are willing to change their tune and try new activities or classes, and balance muscle-building with endurance activities. We all fall into the trap of repeating the same workouts week after week, which can set you up for injury or boredom."

—Dan Timm, Aria Spa & Club

Posture-Perfect Plié

Ever dreamed of having the strong, graceful body of a ballet dancer? When you replace barbells with barre-work, it doesn't take long to reap the benefits: lean abs, firm buttocks, a flat tummy, and slim thighs. Add in perfect posture, improved flexibility, balance, and coordination, and you can't lose. The plié, which literally means "the fold," is often the first ballet move dance students learn. Try it yourself to tone and stretch your legs and perfect your posture.

inspiration

BalletSport!

COOLFONT RESORT, CONFERENCE CENTER, HEALTH SPA
BERKELEY SPRINGS, WV

At Coolfont Resort's BalletSport! program, teens develop their physique with ballet-inspired exercises and powerful dance routines. Ballet benefits the entire body because it requires overall muscular control, whether you are holding an arabesque or leaping through the air. BalletSport! also works on the core body and specific muscle groups that run up and down the spine and stomach. These are key to achieving balance throughout the rest of the body. Although it takes years of training to achieve the perfectly conditioned body of a prima ballerina, everyone can benefit by incorporating ballet moves into their exercise routine. "Our class is like 'Swan Lake' meets Muscle Beach," says Yvonne Salcedo Williams, a former dancer and director of the program.

BalletSport!

✶ **Slouch buster.** At least three times a day, stop what you're doing and pay attention to the way you're standing. Becoming aware of your posture is the fastest way to get in the habit of walking tall. Try giving yourself a little reminder, like a silk ribbon tied loosely around your wrist.

Here's How...

MUST HAVES

- comfortable clothes
- soft piano or ballet music (optional)
- mirror in which you can watch yourself (optional)

1. Stand in front of a mirror with your feet a little wider than shoulder-width apart, toes pointing directly outward toward the opposite walls. Let your arms hang loosely at your sides.
2. Straighten your back and visualize a vertical beam going in a line from the tip of your head to the base of your spine. Imagine that there is energy running up and down the beam, and that you are pushing up the ceiling with the top of your head.
3. Flatten your stomach muscles and tuck your tailbone in slightly. Make sure your weight is centered over your feet.
4. Slowly bend your knees until your thighs are perpendicular to your shins, making sure not to extend your knees beyond your feet. (Hint: only your legs should be bending—your upper half should still be straight and strong.)
5. Keeping your abs tight and your back straight, slowly straighten your legs and return to the original position, being careful not to pop up quickly. As you do this, continue to visualize yourself holding up the ceiling with the top of your head. Repeat 10 times.

"If one word could sum up the collective quest of BalletSport! it would be 'posture'. In the pursuit of a svelte body, students learn that the spine supports all aspects of health. You should be aware of your spine and posture at all times. Pretend there is a string from the crown of the head to the tailbone that aligns you from head to toe."

—Yvonne Salcedo Williams, BalletSport! instructor

✴ **Sitting pretty.** When you're sitting at your desk in class, keep both feet planted on the ground with your back resting lightly on the chair. Whenever you think of it (remember that ribbon!) pull your abs back and in for 10 seconds at a time, breathing normally. This not only helps you sit up straight, it also tones your abs.

Home Stretch

Cardio and strength training may look impressive, but don't forget to stretch. Regular stretching is as important to staying in good shape as lifting weights and working up a sweat. Studies show that tacking on even a simple flexibility sequence like this one at the end of your routine helps prevent injury, improves posture, and gives you 20 percent more strength-building bang for your workout.

inspiration

Stride and Stretch

KRINSKY/CANYON RANCH YOUNG ADULT SUMMER PROGRAM
BRYN MAWR COLLEGE
PHILADELPHIA, PA

At this summer camp, teens choose from over 100 activities to tone and strengthen the body and jump-start themselves into a healthy way of life. There are sports, nutrition, and cooking classes, and even classes in creative writing and journaling. The Stride and Stretch class concentrates on stretching the core body as it elongates muscles, relieves body tension, eases pain and soreness, and corrects muscle imbalance. It will even improve posture, which is especially good for those teens who spend way too many hours hunched over a computer.

Krinsky/Canyon Ranch Young Adult Summer Program

✱ **Swing slow.** Anytime you stretch, it's important to breathe deeply and move slowly. Avoid jerky or bouncy motions, which can cause a sprain, and try instead to let the muscle lengthen in a controlled, gradual way. And as with any exercise, if something hurts, stop.

Here's How...

MUST HAVES
- loose-fitting clothes
- comfortable place to stretch out

HAM-FLEX KNEE PULL
Stretches: hamstrings and lower back

1. Start out lying on your back, knees bent, feet flat on the floor. Lift one foot off the floor, and bring your knee toward your chest, pulling it gently with both hands. Hold for 15 to 30 seconds, then release the leg and repeat with the other leg.

2. Now repeat the same exercise with each leg, but this time straighten the stationary leg flat on the floor as you bring the other knee toward your chest. Keep the leg on the floor as straight as you can. Hold for 15 to 30 seconds.

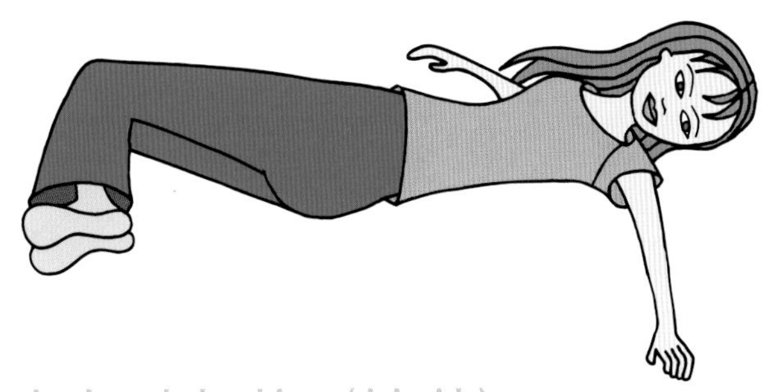

BODY TWIST
Stretches: upper back and shoulders (deltoids)

Lie on your back with both knees bent and your feet flat on the floor. Extend your arms out to the side, palms facing down. Let both knees drop to the left and turn your head the opposite way. Hold for at least 30 seconds, then roll back up to center. Repeat on the right side.

"Flexibility is one of the most often neglected, mis-prescribed, and crucially important elements of fitness. Recent research suggests that it is just as important to not be over-flexible in certain joints as it is to be flexible in others. Flexibility needs are uniquely personal and depend upon the individual anatomical structure of each person. At Canyon Ranch, we recommend that you seek the advice of a qualified professional in order to develop an appropriate and personal flexibility program."

—Nicholas Sita, Ph.D., Krinsky/Canyon Ranch Young Adult Summer Program

BE-THE-BOW STRETCH
Stretches: front of thighs (quadriceps)

Lie on your left side with your left arm stretched out above you and your head resting on your left arm. Reach back with your right hand and grab your right ankle. (If you can't quite reach your ankle, just grab your sock instead.) Stay in that position, keeping your head down, for 15 to 20 seconds. Switch and do the other side.

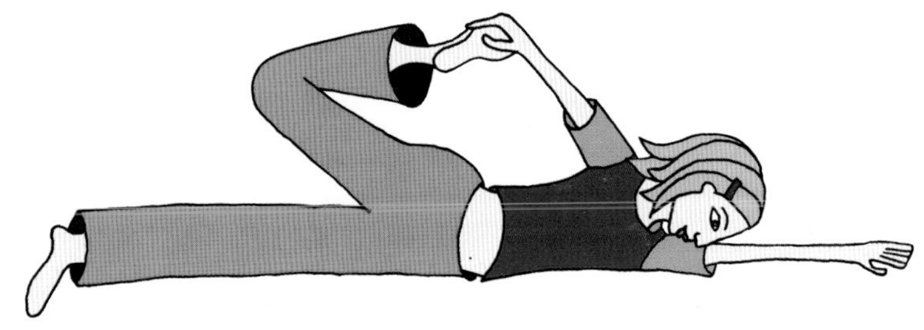

✷ **Solo stretch.** Flexibility training is for more than just the end of a workout. Even on days when you don't have time or can't muster the energy to work up a sweat, take 10 minutes to stretch in front of the TV. This keeps you limber and helps release tension on days you don't exercise.

Red Rock Lettuce Wraps

You exercise, get lots of sleep, and drink tons of water. So how come you're tired, grumpy, and broken out? The problem may be what you're eating. Foods loaded with sugar and flour may give you an instant energy boost, but it won't be long before that boost goes bust, and your mood starts swinging faster than a seesaw. Even worse, these foods trigger a response in your body that makes you crave even more of the same. Before your evil twin grabs for the junk, treat yourself to a hearty chicken salad wrap. This healthy snack from Utah's Red Mountain Spa is not only totally delicious, it will give you the fuel you need to get through the day.

inspiration

School for Adventure Cuisine

RED MOUNTAIN SPA
ST. GEORGE, UT

At the Red Mountain Spa, Chef Chad Luethje advises teens to bag the junk food and take back control by cooking up healthy alternatives to favorite pig-out foods. Some of the culinary tricks taught at Red Mountain's four-day cooking class include substituting whole grains for white flour as you knead bread like a pro and creating crisp fruit snacks to put the spring back in your step.

Red Mountain Spa

✱ **Fuel up.** With all of the physical (and emotional!) ups and downs you go through as a teen, it's especially important to make sure you have a balanced diet. To keep your mood lifted and your energy high, space your meals evenly throughout the day. Hold off temptation in the long stretches between meals by having wholesome snacks on hand.

Here's How...

1. Drain the water from the chicken, then place the chicken in a mixing bowl. Add the lime juice, celery, cilantro, green onion, and mayonnaise.

2. Mix it up until it's a little creamy and holds together. Season with lemon pepper and tabasco sauce.

3. Arrange 2 lettuce leaves on each plate, and top each leaf with chicken salad, cucumber, and tomato. Wrap the lettuce leaf around the salad and enjoy.

Makes 4 servings, each with 117 calories, 4 grams of fat, and 14 grams of protein.

MUST HAVES

- 6 ounces grilled chicken breast, diced
- squeeze of fresh lime juice
- 1 stalk of celery, rinsed and chopped
- 1 tablespoon cilantro, rinsed and chopped
- 1 tablespoon green onion, chopped
- 2 tablespoons lite mayonnaise
- lemon pepper to taste
- dash of tabasco sauce
- 8 lettuce leaves, 2 per plate
- 1/2 cucumber, cut into half-moon wheels
- 2 tomatoes, cut into wedges

"It's important for teens to immerse themselves in healthy cooking and healthy eating, not just to read their scales every morning or go on starvation diets. We're more about inspiring them to climb a mountain and run a distance they've never reached before."

—Deborah Evans, Red Mountain Spa

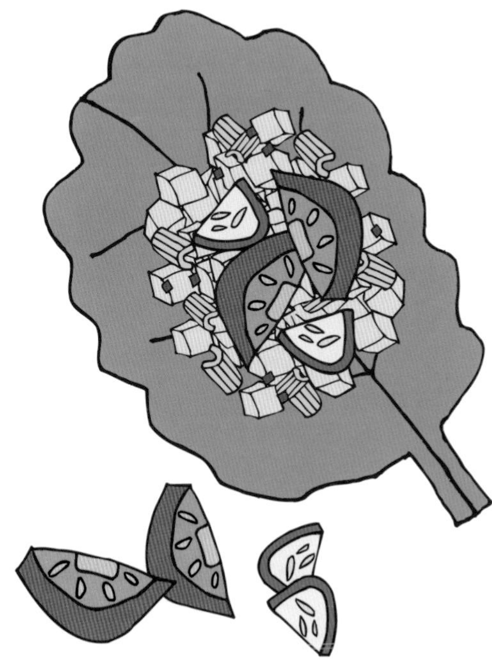

✷ **Accept no substitutes.** If you're (wisely) cutting down on sugar, keep away from foods that contain substitute sweeteners like aspartame and phenylalanine. These chemicals can be even worse for you than sugar, and they keep your body on the same roller coaster of snacking, crashing, and craving more. Try stevia instead, an all-natural, chemical-free sweetener that has no effect on cravings. Or, better yet, satisfy hunger with heartier choices like beans, vegetables, and whole grains like brown rice.

Self-Soother Massage

If you're an athlete, odds are you know a thing or two about muscle aches. After a day on the sports field, there is nothing better to soothe soreness than a massage. Take relaxation into your own hands with a do-it-yourself muscle soother. Whether you're sore from sports or just feeling tense, a self-treatment lets you focus your attention on the places where your body needs it most. The next time tightness kicks in, find a quiet place, lie down on the floor, and try this technique.

inspiration

Teen Sports Massage

PHANTOM HORSE ATHLETIC CLUB & SPA
POINTE SOUTH MOUNTAIN RESORT
PHOENIX, AZ

The therapists at Phantom Horse Athletic Club & Spa have turned sports massage into an art form. The spa's Teen Sports Massage is not only intended to make you feel better, but can also be used to help prevent injuries, get the body limber for the playing field, and keep it in optimal condition.

The therapists also help athletes recover from injuries, zeroing in on specific aches and pains, and massaging in a penetrating gel at the points that need special attention. They also concentrate on pressure points in the body that are said to unlock other muscle groups. Therapists will either "knead" or "push," depending on what is required. Massage keeps muscles soft, elongated, and open. Having loose, open muscles creates balance in the body and, in turn, promotes overall wellness.

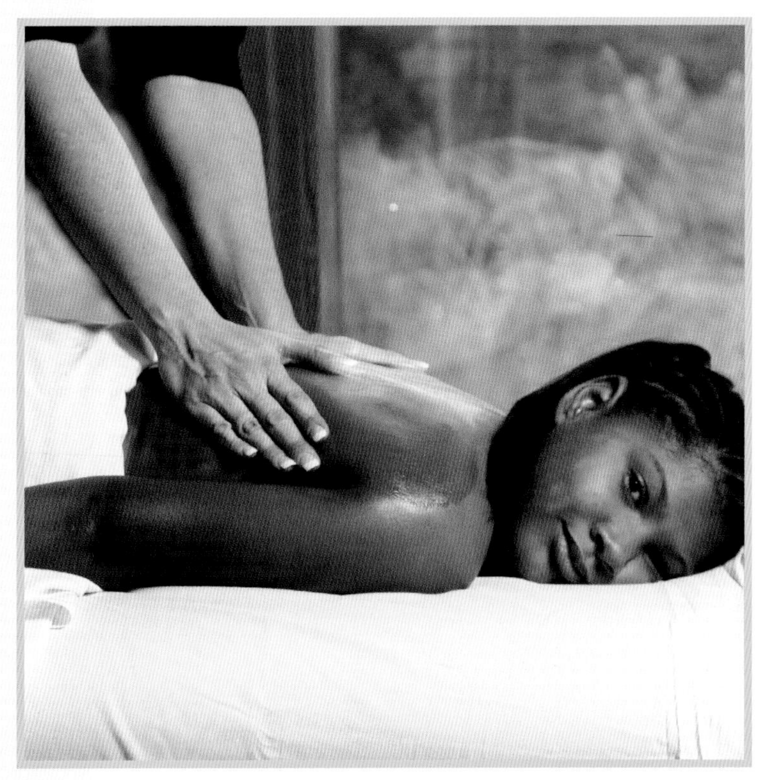

Phantom Horse Athletic Club & Spa

✳ **Now ear this.** If stress sneaks in when you're out and about, try this quick ear fix: Place one hand on each ear, and gently pull the sides straight outward. Repeat 3 times. Now do it again, but this time, pull gently straight up, then straight down. (And as a yoga instructor would tell you, don't forget to breathe!)

Here's How...

MUST HAVES

- loose-fitting clothes
- comfortable place to stretch out

ARMS

1. Place your left hand on the muscle on the front of your upper arm (the biceps), so your thumb points up toward your head. Use your thumb to firmly stroke the muscle upward toward your shoulder. Repeat on the other side.

2. Bend your right arm at 90 degrees, with your hand resting on your stomach. Place your left hand on the muscle on the back of your right arm (the triceps). Press firmly into your triceps muscle, and gradually work your way down toward your elbow (it helps to straighten your right arm as you go). Repeat 3 times, then do the other side.

LEGS

1. Press the fingers of both hands into the top of your right thigh (the quadriceps). Slide your hands gradually down your thigh to the kneecap. Repeat 3 times, to cover the whole thigh and completely relax the muscles, then switch to the other side.

2. Place your right foot over your left knee. Use both hands to grab your right thigh, and press your fingers into the back of your leg (the hamstrings). Slowly work your hands up your thigh, pressing firmly as you go. Repeat 3 times, and then switch sides.

3. Bend your right leg, and hold your calf muscle with both hands. Press down with your thumbs as you slide your hands up your calf to your knee. Repeat 3 times, then switch sides.

NECK

The base of your skull has two powerful pressure points (known as the occipital ridge) that send messages down the spinal column to relax your whole body. Begin by putting 2 tennis balls in a sock, and tie the end. Lie down on your back, place the sock under your neck so the balls are pressed against the skull ridge, right above the two hollow spots. Relax for 20 minutes in this position.

"Athletes often think of massages for soreness, but preventative sports massage is done to help prevent serious athletic injury. It helps to warm up the muscles, stretching them and making them flexible for optimal athletic performance. It also stimulates the flow of blood and nutrients to the muscles, reduces muscle tension, loosens the muscles, and produces a feeling of psychological readiness."

—Bill Price, Phantom Horse Athletic Club & Spa

✶ **Meltdown.** Applying heat is one of the most effective cures for soreness. If you're still feeling the burn long after your workout is over, melt muscle tension by soaking in the tub, or placing a heating pad over the area.

✶ **Wash it away.** A good rubdown releases toxins that your muscles have been holding onto. After a massage, help your body sweep out the junk by drinking lots of water.

Snack Attack

School's out. You just got home, slung your backpack onto the floor, and kicked off your shoes. After a hard day of tests, school bells, and yakking to your friends, you are starving and can't wait to hit the fridge. Instead of fast-food burgers, try fueling up with nutritious, great-tasting snacks. You will be full until dinner, and the added benefits of more energy and better concentration will help get homework done faster.

inspiration

Easy, Awesome Snacks

PRITIKIN LONGEVITY CENTER® & SPA
AVENTURA, FL

Fad diets come and go, but the Pritikin Longevity Center® & Spa has been the vacation choice for weight loss and wellness for thousands worldwide for more than 30 years. Teens are welcome year-round, and especially enjoy the Pritikin Family Program, held summers at the waterfront resort. A typical morning includes tennis lessons, cooking classes featuring awesome snacks, burritos, and fruit smoothies, and nutrition workshops packed with real eye-openers. As one teen said: "That's what's happening to my arteries?" Afternoons are spent exercising with Cardio Blast Workouts, weight lifting, and going to the beach. Evenings, it's swimming under the stars at the resort's pool. Pritikin participants report tangible results which are scientifically documented in more than 100 studies published in top medical journals.

Pritikin Longevity Center® & Spa

✳ **Snack stash.** Keep the glove compartment of your car stocked with healthy, nutritious snacks like nuts, trail mix, and fruit like apples and bananas.

Here's How...

Grocery goods. If you are out and about, try a grocery store for a quick, wholesome snack. Many stores now have extensive salad bars and deli counters with healthy choices like low-salt, fresh-roasted turkey breast. The produce section has fruit and single-serving plastic containers of pre-cut, ready-to-eat fruit like watermelon and cantaloupe.

Smooth smoothie. At home, whip up your own awesome smoothie. It's easy! In the blender, put 1 cup of fruit-flavored nonfat yogurt, 1 sliced banana, 1 cup of crushed ice, and about 1/2 cup orange juice. Blend until it's mouth-wateringly smooth.

Make it pop. Pop up some good taste with low-fat, low-calorie popcorn. Your best bet is to use a hot-air popcorn popper. Some microwave brands are also good choices. Look for "low-fat" or "94-percent fat-free" varieties. Got a sweet tooth? Add a dash of cinnamon sugar and some dried fruit to your popcorn. Want spice? Try a dash of garlic or chili powder. Or make your own tasty popcorn trail mix. Add dried fruit like raisins, nuts such as soy nuts and almonds, or sunflower seeds.

Think fast. Your friends insisting on fast food? No problem. Try the many new salads now available (just steer clear of the cheesy varieties and full-fat dressings). Order grilled chicken sandwiches (without the mayo). If available, order a baked potato and top it with zesty salsa. Another good choice: corn on the cob. And many chains now offer nutritious and delicious desserts, such as fruit and yogurt parfaits and apples with yogurt dip.

Party hearty. Having friends over this weekend? Instead of ordering the same old greasy pizza, plan a build-your-own-burrito party. Line up all the fixings in separate festive plates—warm tortillas, cooked ground turkey breast, cooked kidney and black beans, low-fat shredded cheese, salsa, sliced lettuce, and guacamole—and watch the fun unfold!

"We see phenomenal results among teens. UCLA scientists found that weight loss averages 10 pounds in two weeks for kids needing to lose weight; LDL 'bad' cholesterol falls an average 34%; and blood pressure plummets from pre-hypertension to normal levels. And they have a great time. Our teenage guests tell us: 'I had no idea healthy living could be so easy and fun!'"

—Paul Lehr, President, Pritikin Longevity Center® & Spa

✳ **An old favorite.** A P, B & J sandwich gets much healthier if you use 100-percent whole-wheat bread (it should say whole wheat in the ingredients list, not just wheat) and 100-percent pure fruit preserves. If you're a banana lover, use bananas instead of jam. Arrange your banana slices right on top of the peanut butter.

CAN'T ... S MA ... UP

BEA

BROW KNOW-HOW

BOO

GLAM-SLAM NAILS

UTY

-UP AIR CO OR

OME BEAUTY BAR

STERS

TAT YO HENNA

Everyone needs a special beauty boost now and again. We're talking about bonus treatments that go above and beyond your everyday routine—the ones that take you from ordinary to extraordinary. Beauty boosters like these are a spa specialty, and we've got the goods for your own at-home makeover marathon.

Why not let your fingers do the talking with a Glam-Slam manicure that's truly unique? Or how about a makeup lesson from the pros for your best look ever? Get the scoop on tweezing those untamed brows, or show off your artistic side with a hip henna tattoo. Now hear this! Your locks need love, too. Our Head-Over-Heels Scalp Rub will make both your head *and* your hair happy. And if an extra spark is what you're after, crank up the volume with our Turn-It-Up Hair Color. We're betting these lavish luxuries will give you a great confidence boost—and have everyone singing your praises.

Gloss 'n' Go Hair Pack

Hair needs pampering, too. Sun, styling, even extreme temperatures can take the life out of your crowning glory. This intensive treatment is loaded with gloss-enhancing protein and moisture, plus baking soda to dissolve any dulling residue. After 30 minutes of this power pack, you'll be turning heads with your super-shiny mane.

inspiration

Gloss

AVON SALON & SPA
NEW YORK, NY

At Avon Salon & Spa, clients emerge tossing lustrous locks. Avon's for-teens-only shine/color treatment, called Gloss, is all about restoring vitality to your hair.

The treatment begins with a scalp massage that stimulates blood circulation and promotes growth. The stylist then applies the gloss mixture, letting you pick between either a clear application or a semi-permanent color of your choice. The solution coats your hair with a gentle, restorative formula that won't damage your locks. The gloss works especially well for dry, brittle hair and hair that has been dulled by relaxers, hair straighteners, or harsh dyes.

Avon Salon & Spa

✻ **Vinegar lift.** Apple cider vinegar is much more than a salad dressing—it's an instant rejuvenator that washes away product build-up. If your hair feels dull from months of gel, mousse, and heavy conditioners, keep it shiny and residue-free with a weekly rinse in 1 cup of cider vinegar.

Here's How...

MUST HAVES

- 2 eggs
- 1/2 cup mayonnaise (if your hair is extra-long, make it 3/4 cup)
- 1 tablespoon baking soda
- plastic shower cap
- medium-size bath towel

1. Beat the eggs until smooth. Add the mayo and baking soda, mixing well to combine.
2. Toss a towel in the dryer on high heat for 5 to 10 minutes.
3. Use your hands to scoop the mixture onto your dry hair and scalp, working it thoroughly in from roots to ends.
4. Cover your head with the shower cap, and then wrap your head in the hot towel. (Heat helps the formula penetrate the hair shaft more effectively, so your hair can absorb all those hydrating nutrients.)
5. Let the mixture sit on your hair for 30 minutes. Then rinse thoroughly, shampoo, and condition as usual.
6. When it's time to rinse for the last time, use cool water to seal the hair shaft and make it extra shiny.

"The biggest problem teens have with hair is damage caused by straightening. They don't realize how much that strips the moisture, and they show up here with that little line of breakage framing their face."

—Jackie Laraia, Avon Salon & Spa

✶ **Pretty sweet.** If your hair's especially damaged, add 1/4 cup of honey to the mix. Honey helps restore lost moisture, body, and shine to damaged tresses—and it rinses out easily, even though it's sticky.

Glam-Slam Nails

For those who dare to be different, a one-of-a-kind nail design can showcase the true you. Indulge your creative spirit as you transform your nails into an artistic display. Nail polish is a perfect medium for painting flowers, zebra stripes, leopard spots, or new creations all your own. Look to nature for inspiration, and your manicure will become your masterpiece.

inspiration

Be-jewelled

THE PRIMA DONNA SPA FOR TEENS
ALLEGRIA SPA
PARK HYATT BEAVER CREEK
BEAVER CREEK, CO

Fingernail art is the rave at the Prima Donna Spa for Teens, a part of the Allegria Spa. Prima Donna's Be-jewelled includes shimmer, glitter, and fake rhinestones. Its nail bar also features whimsical decals to inspire you: daisies, hibiscus, butterflies, and monograms.

This unique approach to the traditional manicure starts with a thorough cleaning, and a chocolate-whip hand mask to soften the skin. Guests pick from a paint box of colors and top their choice of polish with glitter and gold, a wild 'n' crazy decal, or hand-painted artwork. Try stripes or polka dots, or go for something simple like alternating bright colors on each finger. Whatever mood you are in—go for it. You can be artsy, edgy, or playful—it's all at your fingertips. For fancy feet, you can also try the Twinkle Toes treatment.

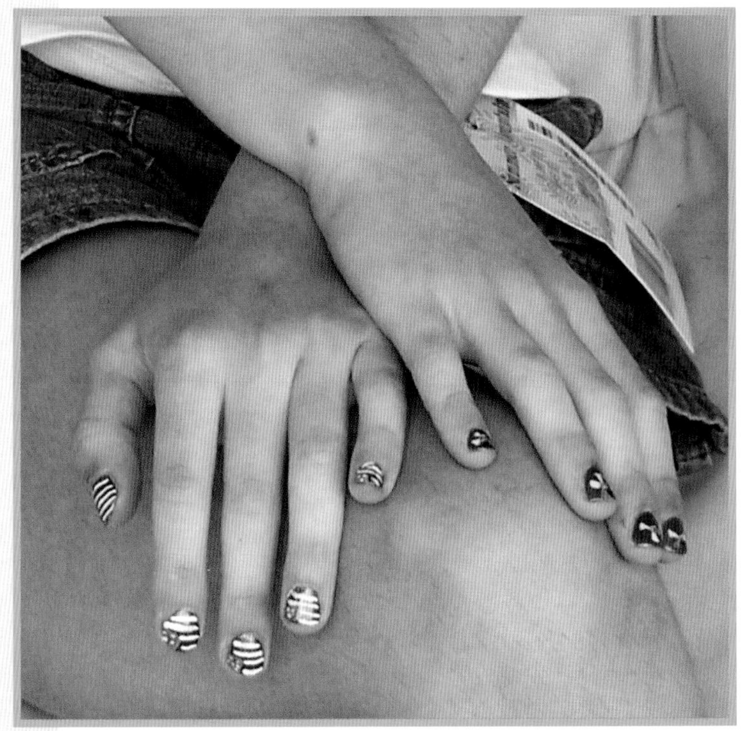

The Prima Donna Spa for Teens

* **Salon style.** Decals and stencils (available at most beauty supply stores) let you decorate your nails the easy way. If painting's not your thing, shop around to see what's out there.

Here's How...

1. Use the nail polish remover and cotton balls to remove any leftover polish from cuticles and nail beds. File nails to achieve the shape you like best.

2. Soak your fingers in warm, soapy water for 5 minutes. Use the nailbrush to wash away any dirt from under your nails.

3. Dry your hands thoroughly. Apply a base coat in the first color and allow to dry (10 to 15 minutes should do it).

4. This second coat is where you can really get creative. Use the brush to paint designs in whatever other colors, shapes, and themes you like. (To keep the colors from mixing together, rinse the brush well when switching between bottles.)

5. Wait at least 10 minutes for nails to dry, then finish with a clear top coat to protect your finished art.

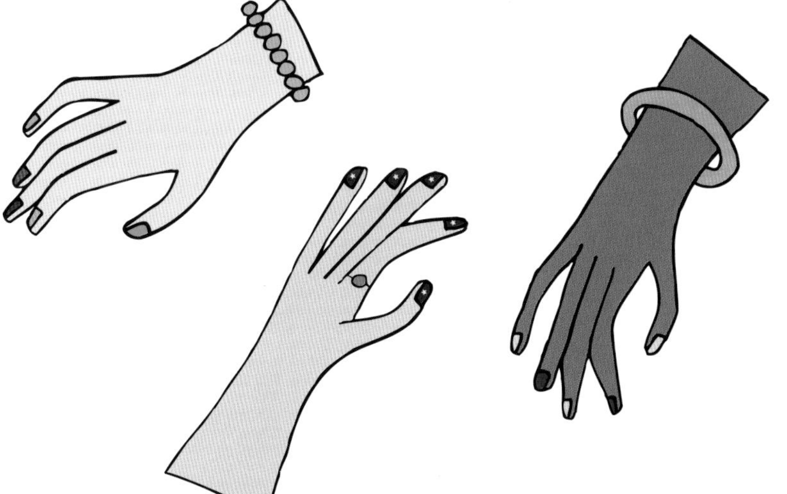

✳ **Turn up the volume.** To make your designs extra-bright and long-lasting, use water-based acrylic paint instead of polish for the second coat. Acrylic paint colors are super-saturated and let you really make a statement.

MUST HAVES

- non-acetone nail polish remover
- cotton balls
- emery board
- bowl of warm, soapy water
- nailbrush
- small-tip paintbrush
- nail polish in multiple colors (at least 2, but you can use as many as 10)
- clear top coat
- water-based acrylic paint and glitter dust (optional)

Inspiration Central

Here are a few more inspiring ideas to help you dream up your own perfect 10:

Color cue. For a funky twist that's fast and easy, gather up 10 different base coat shades, and paint each nail a different color. Once that dries, you can paint your designs on top. (Hint: If you're using multiple base colors, keep your top designs simple and consistent so the effect still looks polished.)

Split personality. Try this half-and-half approach to polish: Follow steps 1 to 3, then paint the left half of each nail in another color. You can finish either with a top coat, or paint more details for added drama.

Glitter glam. Sprinkle glitter dust over small circles of wet polish to make sparkly dots.

Ripple effect. Get a swirling, marbled look by applying spots of color over the base coat, then flicking your hands from side to side to make the shades run together.

Can't-Miss Makeup

The key to gorgeous makeup is that it highlights, rather than changes, the natural features that make you unique. Choose the right shades for your skin, and use them in the way that best suits your mood. No matter what the latest trend, the secret of true beauty is always the same: Be who you are. Make this your mantra in love, life, and lipstick, and you'll never go wrong.

inspiration

Makeup Lesson

TEENSPA
MALL OF AMERICA
BLOOMINGTON, MN

At TeenSpa, top makeup pros and stylists show you how to emphasize your eyes, play down your blemishes, and create a romantic, "just blushed" look. They will even teach you how to get ready for a date with their secret shortcuts to beauty.

Teens meet one-on-one with a makeup artist who evaluates their skin type and tone, and then helps them create a daily makeup routine that lets their individual style shine. Professionals encourage teens to stick with a subtle, natural look for everyday wear, and save the smoky eyes and dark lipstick for special evening occasions. The makeup artist will usually do half the face, then coach the teens to do the other half themselves, so they can re-create the look at home. Each person leaves with a personalized cheat sheet, as well as the makeup essentials used during the lesson.

TeenSpa

* **A light touch.** Forget the painted-lady look. Remember that the goal is to enhance, not hide, the true you. Use a light touch with everything and when in doubt, leave it out.

Here's How...

1. Wash your skin and apply a dab or two of moisturizer. (If your face is prone to breakouts, use a light, oil-free version.)

2. Use your fingers to dab concealer under each eye up to the lower lash line, and on any blemishes. Pat gently until thoroughly blended.

3. Using a fluffy makeup brush, apply loose powder over your face. This sets your concealer and helps the blush go on more smoothly. (Hint: After you dip your brush, tap the handle lightly to shake off any extra powder before applying.)

4. Tame unruly brows with a comb, then apply a clear brow gel to set them in place.

5. Follow the tips below to create the look you want.

MUST HAVES

- moisturizer
- concealer stick
- matte loose powder and fluffy brush
- brow comb or dry toothbrush
- clear brow gel
- powder blush and brush
- eye shadow brush
- 2–3 eye shadows in a range of tones
- 1–2 shades of sheer lip gloss and brush
- lip liner
- eyeliner
- mascara

"Blush seems easy to apply, but there is a trick to getting it in exactly the right place to best accentuate the cheekbones. As an everyday rule of thumb, draw an imaginary diagonal line from the center of each eye to the bottom of the nose, then back to each ear. That is the area where the blush should go. Always apply blush in sweeping motions, using a large brush."

—Stacey Ackerman, TeenSpa

Need a special look? Here's how to do it ...

	ROMANTIC	GLAMOROUS
 **Eyes** 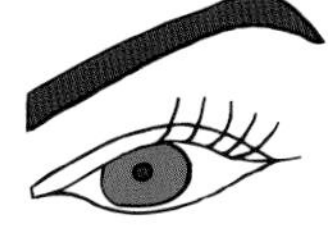	Sweep a matte beige shadow over the lid from lash line to brow bone. Then use a soft brown or taupe from the lash line to the crease. Apply dark brown mascara from the base of your lashes to the tip. (Avoid the gunky look—keep it to one coat.)	Apply a neutral matte shadow (like cream or beige) over the whole lid, from lash line to brow bone. Then apply a shimmery gold or pink just from the lash line to the crease. Finish with a darker color (like a shimmery bronze or plum) only in the crease. Use black mascara from the base of your lashes to the tips. Then apply a brown or charcoal-colored eyeliner just above your lash line on the upper lids.
Cheeks 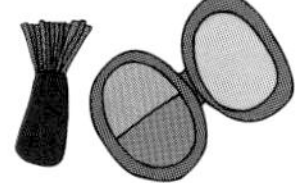	Smile. See the center of your cheek's apple? This is where your blush starts. Use the brush to apply a warm, earthy-toned powder blush out to your hairline, blending so there are no edges.	Use a powder blush in warm peach or soft pink. To pump up the glam, sweep the blush into the hollows of your cheeks (suck your cheeks in to find the hollows) and blend out to hairline.
Lips 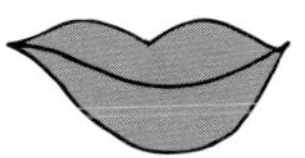	For a natural look, apply a sheer lipstick or tinted gloss first, then define and fill in the lips with the liner. Blend with the lip brush to get rid of any edges.	For a fuller effect, use two different glosses—one darker shade all over, and then a lighter shade in the center of the lower lip. Use a soft berry-toned lip liner to define the outer edges of your lips, then use a lip brush to blend.

Tattoo-You Henna

Get hip to henna! Henna body painting is an ancient art traced back to Turkey in 7,000 B.C. and practiced all over the Middle East and India today. Henna, known as *mendhi* in northern India, is a tall, shrub-like plant that grows in hot, dry climates. The leaves are ground into a powder and made into a paste, which is then used to stain the skin. This recipe gives you temporary tattoos with serious staying power. Paint posies on your hands, swirl curlicues on your toes—whatever shows the world what a work of art you really are.

inspiration

Henna Tattoo

THE SPAHHHT YOUTH SPA
THE HYATT REGENCY HILL COUNTRY RESORT AND SPA
SAN ANTONIO, TX

The SPAhhhT Youth Spa

Traditionally reserved for weddings and rituals, henna tattoos can add a boost to any outfit, and help you look your best even when you don't have a royal engagement. At SPAhhhT, the master henna artist doesn't take a cookie-cutter approach to design—each teen walks away with original henna artwork. Get butterflies near your belly button to show off in a bikini, Spiderman's web down your arms for the next costume party, or a simple flower on your ankle for a soft, romantic look. The tattoos last about 10 days to two weeks, and stay vibrant as long as you don't scrub them too hard in the shower.

* **Tattoo trivia.** In India, where henna body painting goes back thousands of years, the art form was an important part of wedding rituals. Today, young brides still have their hands and feet decorated by the older women as they listen to words of wisdom for a happy marriage.

Here's How...

MUST HAVES

- 1 cup water
- 2 teabags of black tea
- 2 tablespoons whole cloves
- juice of 1 lemon or lime (or equivalent in juice concentrate)
- 3 tablespoons henna powder —go for the green, not yellow (henna powder is available online and at Indian grocery stores)
- ceramic bowl
- plastic spoon
- paintbrush

1. Put the water, cloves, and tea in a saucepan. Boil until the water is reduced by half. Drain and set aside.
2. Place the henna powder in a small ceramic bowl, and use the plastic spoon to stir in the lemon juice. Gradually add some of the tea mixture, stirring well until you get it to a thick, pasty consistency. Set aside the remaining tea mixture for later.
3. Cover the henna mix with plastic wrap and store it in a dark place for at least 6 hours. (Be sure to use it within the next 24 hours to get the full effect.)
4. Right before you start to tattoo, slowly add the remaining tea mixture. This should moisten the henna enough to restore its original paste-like state, so it's easy to apply.
5. Use the paintbrush to apply the henna in different patterns to your skin. For more advanced shapes, you can also use stencils (buy them at an art store, or create your own originals).
6. Let the henna stay on your skin between 1 and 6 hours (the longer you leave it, the more it will soak in). Once the henna is set, wash it off gently with warm water.

"The henna is a wet gel-like substance when the artist applies it to the skin. Many teens are in a hurry and want to leave as soon as the henna is finished being applied. However, it is very important to wait until the gel gets hard and crumbles in order to give the pigment enough time to soak into the skin. After the gel has flaked off, soak the tattoo with lemon juice. Lemon juice contains a special element that helps seal in the color, and the tattoo will last longer."

—Melody Goeken, Hyatt Regency Hill Country Resort and Spa

✶ **Staying power.** To make the tattoo last as long as possible, avoid using harsh soaps or loofahs on henna-stained skin.

✶ **Sweet tip.** To give your henna stain a boost, use lemon sugar to help set your creation. Add 1 tablespoon sugar to half a lemon's worth of juice, and use a popsicle stick to apply it to your skin right after you've painted on the henna.

Home Beauty Bar

Beauty store shelves are piled high with expensive facial cleansers. But some of the most effective cleansers in the world are simple enough to make at home, for pennies. It's easy to set up your own beauty bar, where you and your friends can mix up your own, unique facial cleansers. And since all the ingredients are fresh, you get to skip the pore-clogging preservatives. (Hint: Feel free to mix and match ingredients to create a formula that's truly one of a kind.)

inspiration

Beauty Bar Bonanza

TEENSPA
MALL OF AMERICA
BLOOMINGTON, MN

At TeenSpa in the Mall of America, each teen is given a large container of plain lip-gloss base. Then it's time to go wild with its beauty bar's different glitters, frosts, and flavors. Invent a new combination, or take suggestions from six spa recipes that have already proven to be winners: "Viva Las Vegas," "Minnesota Snow," "Arizona Desert," "Hershey Pennsylvania," "Miami Beach," or "Heart of Dixie." After mixing, pop your concoction in the microwave, and 45 seconds later you have your own personalized lip gloss. Teens can also make customized lotions by adding scents and colors to large jars of plain lotion.

TeenSpa

Other add-ons to try:

* **Vitamin E oil.** The ultimate moisturizer, vitamin E is a key ingredient in many high-quality cosmetics because of its excellent healing properties. Add a teaspoon to your cleanser for an instant moisture drench, or use it alone at night on the delicate skin under your eyes.

For Dry Skin

A moisture-rich wash to hydrate and smooth. (No need to refrigerate.)

MUST HAVES

- 1 teaspoon mild liquid soap
- 2 tablespoons honey
- 1/2 cup olive oil

For Oily/Acne-Prone Skin

A bacteria-fighting formula that leaves skin soft. (Refrigerate for up to 2 weeks.)

MUST HAVES

- 1/2 cup water
- 1/4 cup skim milk
- 1 egg white
- 2 tablespoons baking soda

For Combination Skin

A gentle cleanser for all skin types. (Refrigerate for up to 2 weeks.)

MUST HAVES

- 1/2 cup plain yogurt
- 1 teaspoon canola oil
- 1 1/2 teaspoons fresh lemon juice

Here's How...

1. Place all your ingredients in a bowl, mixing thoroughly.
2. Pour the mixture into a clean jar or other airtight container.
3. Apply a small amount of the mixture to the palm of your hand, and use your fingers to massage it all over your face. Rinse thoroughly with lukewarm water and pat dry.

✱ **Witch hazel.** A natural astringent made from the plant's bark and leaves, witch hazel helps stave off acne-causing bacteria. Adding 3 tablespoons to your cleanser also freshens the skin and leaves it cool and tingly.

✱ **Glycerine.** Many soaps contain glycerine, a sticky liquid that helps retain moisture. Add 2 tablespoons to your cleansing concoction to keep the formula from drying out.

Brow Know-How

Because eyebrows frame your face, they have a big impact on your overall look. From a diva glare to a giggle attack, brows set the stage for your every expression. For big-time brow renovation, definitely see a professional. But if you're just looking for an easy touch-up, these tips should get you going.

inspiration

Brow Shaping

AVON SALON & SPA
NEW YORK, NY

World-famous eyebrow guru Eliza Petrescu, "Queen of the Arch," who runs Eliza's Eyes at Avon Salon & Spa in Manhattan, will show you how to keep your eyebrows groomed and well-proportioned to complement your features and the shape of your face. Avant-garde fashion designers may give their models bushy caterpillar brows one season and sleek arches the next, but there's no need to be a slave to fashion. A pencil-thin line may look great on the runway, but Eliza recommends figuring out how best to highlight your own unique brow shape.

Avon Salon & Spa

* **Short stop.** Avoid the common pitfall of shortening your brows from the outside in. You can thin and trim, but let the brows run their natural length toward your temples.

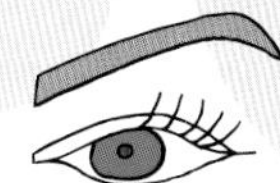

Here's How...

1. To make your brow session as easy as possible, wait until just after you've taken a shower, so your skin is soft and the pores open. (Or just hold a damp washcloth soaked in hot water over the brow area for a few minutes before you begin.) Prep the skin around your brows with a cotton ball soaked in astringent.

2. Remove any stray hairs from between your brows. Using your natural brow line as a guide, tweeze the hairs from below the arch (never from above). The inside edge of your brows should line up with the top of your nose. The end of the arch should line up diagonally at a 45-degree angle to the base of your nose.

3. To trim, brush your brows straight up, using the brow comb or toothbrush. Carefully trim any hair that extends above the top of your natural arch.

MUST HAVES

- astringent
- pair of clean, sharp tweezers (they should allow you to grip the hair firmly without slipping)
- brow comb or dry toothbrush
- sharp eyebrow scissors

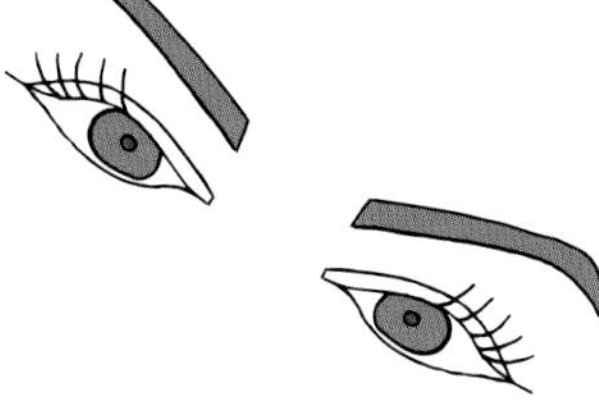

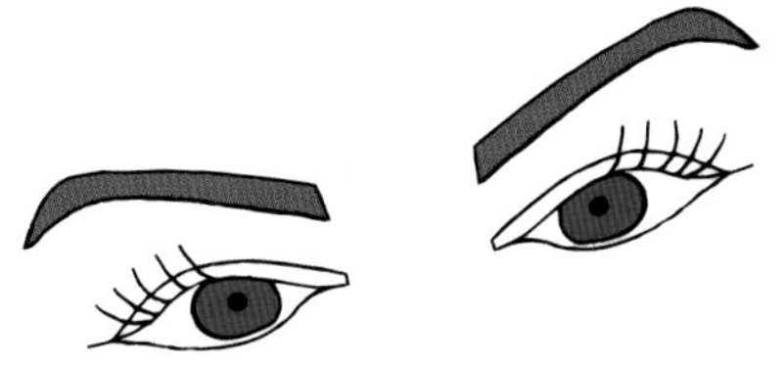

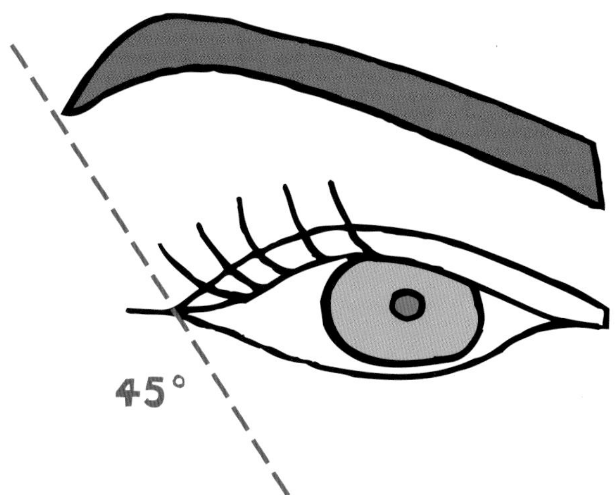

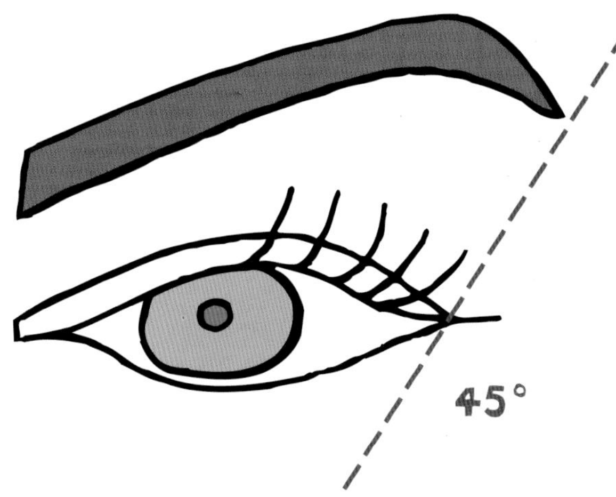

✶ **Hit pause.** It's easy to get carried away as you get the hang of tweezing, so be sure to take frequent breaks and check out your progress. When in doubt, stop. You can always come back and do more tomorrow if you need to.

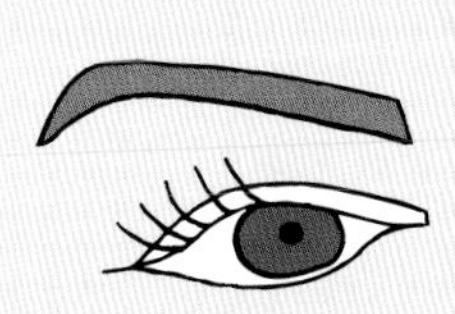

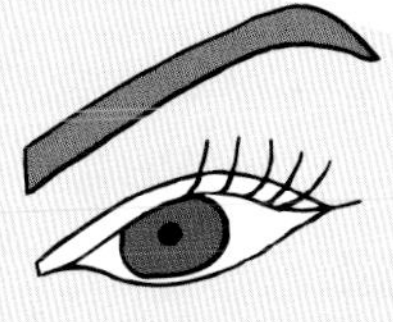

Turn-It-Up Hair Color

Turn up your natural assets with a simple herbal infusion. Whether you want to uncover the gold or rev up the red, your local grocer has all the color-boosting agents you need to take your hair's existing highlights to the next level. The best part about coloring with natural ingredients is that the effects are gradual, which puts you in the driver's seat. The more often you use them, the more dramatic the results.

inspiration

Special Effects

SEVENTEEN STUDIO SPA SALON
PLANO, TX

Bold and beautiful is all the rage at the Seventeen Studio Spa Salon. The salon's hair colorists, who think of themselves as artists, use different types of brushes to highlight hair with streaks and striking splashes of color. The Special Effects hair-coloring service offers such fun-flavored colors as caramel, fudge, and butter-scotch, or brighter hues of blue, hot pink, and copper.

The process starts with a consultation with a color designer, who flips your hair into several different styles to show how the highlights can create a compelling new look. For short hair, try coloring only the tips of the hair to avoid patchy areas. Tie long hair into several ponytails and color only the parts hanging loose for a dramatic "growing-out" look. Feeling really creative? Try zigzag partings on top to define different colors. While waiting for their color to process, teens can chill out and listen to the latest music videos, watch movie trailers, or play games on one of the salon's many computers. After the processing is complete, a restructuring conditioner is applied to seal and protect the color-treated hair.

Seventeen Studio Spa Salon

✳ **Sun-lights.** If you're a blonde or a light brunette, let the sun's rays work their magic the next time you hit the beach: Combine the juice of 1 lemon, 1 tablespoon of sea salt, and 1 cup of water. Pour the mixture into a spray bottle, and spritz it on your hair every few hours to bring out your hair's natural gold.

MUST HAVES

(If you have extra-long locks, double this recipe.)

- color-booster recipe of your choice (see the chart at right)
- 2 cups water
- plastic squeeze bottle (optional)

For gold & honey highlights:

- 1/4 cup loose chamomile tea or dried chamomile flowers
- 1/4 cup chopped fresh rhubarb or loose rhubarb tea

For dark & deep highlights:

- 1/4 cup fresh or dried sage leaves
- 1/4 cup fresh or dried lavender sprigs
- 2 1/2 tablespoons ground cinnamon or 3 cinnamon sticks broken into pieces

For rich & red highlights:

- 1/4 cup dried hibiscus flowers or loose hibiscus tea
- 1/2 cup pure henna powder (Note: Follow instructions on the box; henna is stronger than other herbs and the effects are semi-permanent. Try a sample test first, and start out slow.)

Here's How...

1. Place the herbs in a pot with 2 cups of water. (Hint: Don't use an aluminum pot, because it reacts negatively with the herbs.)
2. Bring to a boil, then reduce the heat and simmer uncovered for 20–25 minutes (until the mixture is reduced by about half).
3. Let cool 10–15 minutes. Then strain out the herbs and pour the mixture into a plastic squeeze bottle. (If you're not using a bottle, just strain it into a bowl.)
4. Shampoo your hair as usual, then use the squeeze bottle (or your hands) to apply the herb mixture to your hair from roots to tips. Rinse well with cool water to seal the hair shaft and help preserve the color.

"Do not shampoo every day! Washing hair too often can strip the hair of the essential oils that help make it strong and healthy. For color-treated hair, washing too much will also make the color fade more quickly. In general, hair is exposed to many chemicals and harsh elements every day, so it is important to protect your hair as much as possible when doing any activity."

—Tiffany Jackson, Seventeen Studio Spa Salon

✳ **Make it last.** To help your new color last, treat your hair to a weekly banana dip. Just mash up an overripe banana and apply it to your hair from roots to tips in place of your regular conditioner.

Head-Over-Heels Scalp Rub

Shiny, silky hair begins with a healthy scalp. Defy the damage caused by blow-drying, sun, and harsh chemicals with a rich, renewing scalp treatment. This aromatic infusion moisturizes your scalp, nourishes your hair, and relaxes body and soul. Try it monthly—weekly if you're extra-dry—for a healthy mane that puts tress-stress on hold and bounces back beautifully.

inspiration

Intensive Scalp Therapy Treatment

THE SPA AT THE CAPE CODDER RESORT
HYANNIS, MA

At the Spa at the Cape Codder Resort, the Intensive Scalp Therapy Treatment is part of a holistic beauty plan. A stylist slathers the crown with an exfoliating mask of algae, setting the head a-tingle, and then vigorously massages the scalp to improve circulation and release toxins. A pampering combination of hot towel wraps is then followed by a douse of warm oils that penetrate the hair shaft and moisturize the scalp. A 10-minute scalp massage leaves locks shiny and bouncy and clients both invigorated and totally relaxed.

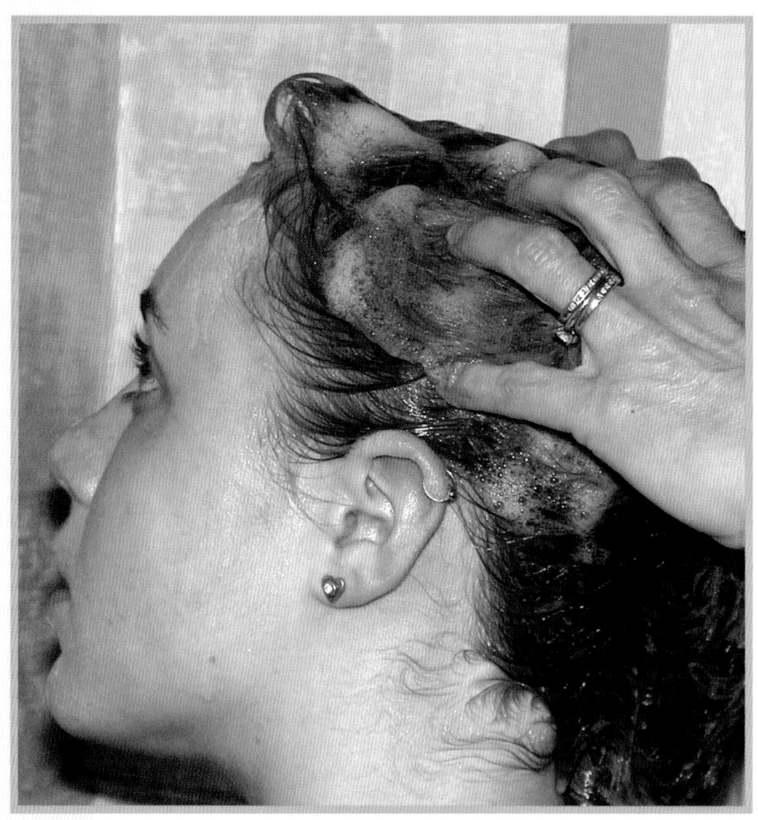

* **Stock up.** Herb-infused oil lasts just as long as regular oil, so you can make a big batch and bottle it for later use. For four months' worth of weekly treatments, increase the ingredients to 8 cups of oil and a full cup of fresh rosemary.

Here's How...

MUST HAVES

- 1/2 cup olive or almond oil
- 1 tablespoon fresh rosemary, chopped
- plastic shower cap

1. Pour the oil into a bowl with the rosemary. Heat in the microwave for 1 or 2 minutes on high (the mixture should be very hot, but not boiling).
2. Allow the oil to cool for 30 minutes. Once it reaches room temperature, strain the oil through a fine sieve or metal coffee filter to remove the rosemary.
3. Gently reheat the oil so it's warm but comfortable to the touch (microwave for about 20 seconds, or just place the bowl in some hot water to heat).
4. Use your fingers to apply the oil little by little to your scalp, parting the hair as you need to. Once the scalp is covered, work more oil along the length of your hair from roots to ends.
5. Massage the oil into your scalp using slow, vigorous circular motions, to boost circulation.
6. Cover your head with a shower cap and leave the oil on your head for 30 minutes.
7. Rinse thoroughly, then shampoo and condition as usual.

"Gentle brushing with a long-bristled plastic brush loosens dead skin and won't make hair oilier or cause undue damage. Cleansing once a week using an extra-strength or clarifying shampoo (a bit stronger than regular shampoo—look for one that's free of oils and fragrances) is also a good beginning for keeping your hair and scalp in good shape."

—Debra Catania, The Spa at the Cape Codder Resort

✴ **Gift tip.** Herb-infused oils make spa-riffic gifts. Try the recipe above with your favorite herb (lavender, mint, sage, and thyme are all great for aromatherapy). Whip up a big batch, funnel it into clear glass bottles, and add a sprig of fresh herbs to each for a festive flourish. Personalize your signature oil with a handmade label.

Ooh-la-la French Manicure

Looking for a polish that can take you from school to prom night? Consider this spin on the classic French manicure. From daytime jeans to evening glam, it's a perfect complement to any getup. While do-it-yourself manicure kits are available at most drugstores, you can get the same effect with this easy technique. Très chic.

inspiration

French Manicure

ASHA SALONSPA
SCHAUMBURG, IL AND CHICAGO, IL

For those who find the classic French manicure a little too conservative, Asha SalonSpa will help you create a personalized color combination. Instead of neutral and white polishes, you can use red with black tips, red with gold tips, or white with silver tips. Let your imagination run wild. During a 45-minute treatment, technicians clip, file, and shape nails and tend to cuticles. After the hands are washed and moisturized, they are given a five-minute reflexology massage. Technicians rub just the right power points to leave hands feeling tingly and relaxed. Then it's time to paint on the base coat and delicately and precisely paint on the tip color.

Asha SalonSpa

* **Cover your bases.** Precision is key to giving yourself a top-notch French manicure, and a base coat is a must. Choose one that not only strengthens the nail but levels out any ridges or imperfections. This creates a smooth surface, so the polish can go on evenly.

Here's How...

1. Use the nail polish remover and cotton balls to remove any leftover polish from your cuticles and nail beds. Once nails are clean, file to your desired shape.

2. Soak your hands in a bowl of soapy water for 5 minutes. Use the nailbrush to remove any dirt from under the nails. Pat dry with a towel.

3. Apply the base coat over your entire nail, and allow 5 minutes to dry.

4. Apply the bottom color (1 or 2 coats), and let dry 15 minutes.

5. Apply the tip color to the top of each nail, following the shape. If your nails are square, paint the line straight across. If they're rounded, hug the curve. As you paint the line of your nail tips, keep them steady by leaning the ball of your painting hand against a hard surface. Place the hand being painted flat against the same surface, so you don't accidentally move and mess up your work. Allow 5 minutes to dry.

6. Apply the clear protective top coat from base to tip, and allow 15 minutes to dry.

"We're having a lot of fun adding this splash of color to the traditional French style, and the girls come in here with swatches from their prom or homecoming dresses, really excited that they are going to have this extra-special look."

—Tracy Vista, Asha SalonSpa

MUST HAVES

- non-acetone nail polish remover
- cotton balls
- bowl of warm, soapy water
- nailbrush
- emery board
- clear protective base coat
- bottom and tip colors (check out the chart for inspiration)
- clear protective top coat

CHOOSE YOUR COLOR COMBO!

	Bottom Color	Tip Color
The Sophisticate	Sheer Pink	White or Cream
The Wild Child	Orange	Royal Blue
The Girly Girl	Pale Pink	Hot Pink
The Dramatic Diva	Dark Wine	White

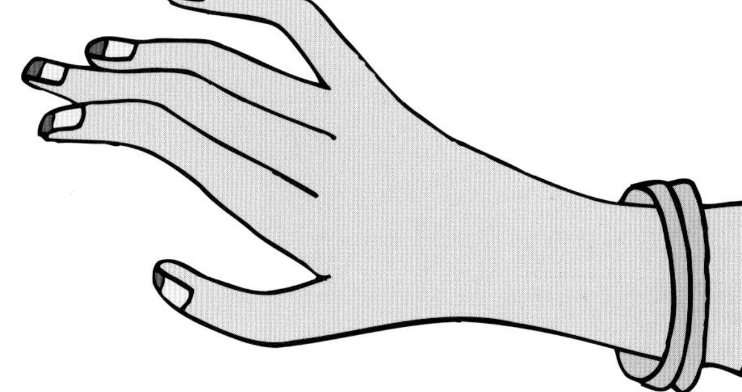

✶ **Tip-top condition.** For extra shine and to protect your tips, be sure to apply the top coat over the entire nail.

STR

OT-ROC RUBDO

HOT COCOA DIP

FEET RETREAT

RELAX-ME REFLEXOLOGY

ESS

ZAPPERS

School, family, friends, relationships—life is a balancing act, and sometimes it's hard to stay steady. Do you run from one thing to the next without a moment to yourself? Do you have trouble focusing, or sleeping soundly? Stress can cause all sorts of health and beauty troubles, ranging from minor breakouts to major headaches. That's the bad news. The good news is, we're here to help!

Soothe tired tootsies with a luscious Feet ReTreat, decompress with a Hot-Rock Rubdown or clear your head with a healing Dream Steam Sinus Remedy. Bitter about boys? Sour about schoolwork? Try a Hot Cocoa Dip bath to sweeten your mood. Armed with all these inSPArational stress releasers, you'll be able to tackle whatever comes your way!

Hot-Rock Rubdown

Hot stone massages are a big bodywork craze—and for good reason: They're one of the most relaxing experiences imaginable. Hot stone therapy draws upon ancient beliefs about the healing powers of rocks and puts them to work with modern massage techniques. After an intense workout or a long day at school, your muscles are ready for a relaxing reward. Since the hot rocks do all the work, you can do this massage either by yourself or with a friend. Mind-centering mission accomplished!

inspiration

Hot Stone Therapy Massage

AVON SALON & SPA
NEW YORK, NY

At Avon Salon & Spa, clients who've had the Hot Stone Therapy Massage say they feel as if they've had a really great warm bath, but with an extra boost. First, the massage therapist applies massage oil with light strokes over the back, arms, and legs to soften the skin and prepare it for the stones. Smooth, heated stones are placed on key pressure points along the body and down the back and legs, on the hands, and even between the toes. The warmth from the rocks deeply penetrates the body as it loosens tight muscles and melts away stress. The therapist uses the stones as well as his/her hands to knead muscles into deep relaxation. The stones are alternately placed and removed during the massage to stimulate and rest the muscles.

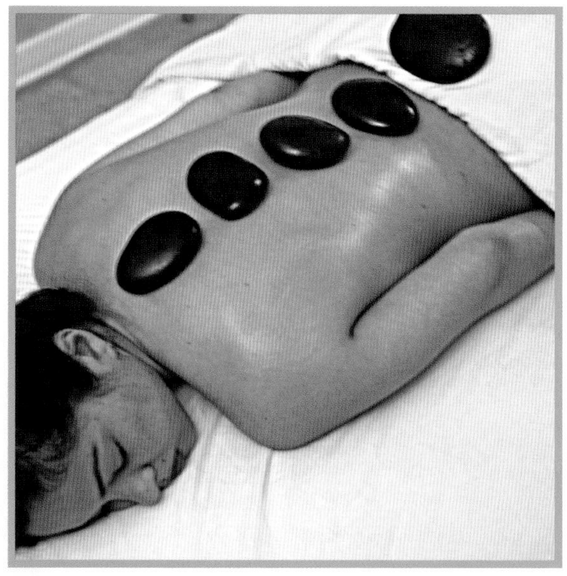

Avon Salon & Spa

✳ **Hot and cold.** Alternating extreme temperatures has been proven to have great benefits for the body. It's very effective to use the relaxing, penetrating heat of warmed stones and then the toning, refreshing chill of cooled stones.

Here's How...

MUST HAVES
- 6 wide, flat stones (around 4 to 6 inches long)
- large bowl (or sink)
- mellow music

1. Collect stones from a pond, river, lake, or the beach, and scrub them down with hot, soapy water.

2. Place the stones in a large bowl or a sink with a drain plug. Fill with hot (but not scalding) tap water, and allow the stones to heat for about 10 minutes. You may need to add more hot water after 5 minutes or so to keep the temperature warm enough. Remove the stones, and dry them thoroughly with a towel.

3. Lie face down on a yoga mat or bed, and breathe deeply. Place one of the stones on your left shoulder, and relax for 2 to 3 minutes as the heat penetrates into the muscle. Remove the stone, and do the same using a new stone on your right shoulder.

4. Repeat these steps on either side of the spine near the middle of your back, and then finish with the last of the warm stones at the base of your lower back.

5. If you have a friend over, use a series of stones at once. Lie on your stomach, and have your friend place 5 or 6 stones down your spine, one in each of your hands, and 3 or 4 down each leg. She can put gentle pressure on the stones, or just leave them there for a few minutes to do their magic. Then warm more stones and switch places so your friend can enjoy the benefits herself.

"A stone therapy massage is a perfect way to break the winter chill. More and more people visit the spa for this treatment during the colder months."

—Ann Marie Comiskey, Avon Salon & Spa

✶ **Just breathe.** To make the most of your massage, finish with a 10-minute meditation. Sit quietly in a comfortable cross-legged position, or roll over onto your back, palms up. Close your eyes, listen to your breath, and let your mind wander where it will.

✶ **D.I.Y. massage oil.** Everyday cooking herbs like rosemary, mint, basil, and sage can help you create the ultimate scented massage experience. Add 1 tablespoon of fresh herbs to 1/2 cup of canola or olive oil, and microwave for 2 minutes. Let the oil cool completely (about 30 minutes), and you have a homemade herbal infusion. Rub it on your back and shoulders before you apply the hot rocks for ultimate back bliss.

Tea Tub With Milk

Milk is great for your body and bones—but if you love the benefits of drinking it, wait until you try bathing in it. The Egyptian queen Cleopatra—one of the legendary knockouts of all time—was renowned for her daily milk baths. Experience this ancient skin-smoothing secret for yourself, and add the calming effects of herbal tea. This creamy tea bath not only leaves you silky-soft, but also infuses your body with scent, warmth, and serenity.

inspiration

Spirulina Milk Bath

GRAND FLORIDIAN SPA & HEALTH CLUB
LA BUENA VISTA, FL

At the Grand Floridian Spa & Health Club, a Spirulina Milk Bath promises to turn moods around as it cleanses and softens the skin. Spirulina, an algae-based liquid, is a powerful protein source, rich in vitamins and minerals. As water jets, glowing candles, and aromatic pillows offer cozy comfort, the silky bathwater warms, soothes, and nourishes the body. A therapist begins body-brushing with a loofah mitt to exfoliate the skin, then massages in healing oils to keep the skin hydrated. The treatment finishes with either a facial and scalp massage, or a foot massage with a choice of healing oil.

Grand Floridian Spa & Health Club

✳ **Tub time.** There's a science to soaking that can promote a profound sense of well-being, says Alex Zink from the Grand Floridian. Fill the tub until almost full, and always soak for at least 20 minutes to get the full sense of bliss. The part of the nervous system that kicks it into the comfort zone needs at least that much time to wind down.

Here's How...

1. Combine all ingredients except the milk, and heat them on the stove or in the microwave until just boiling. Allow the mixture to steep for several hours or overnight.

2. Draw a warm bath, and add the milk. Using a strainer to separate the solids, pour the fully steeped mixture into the tub.

3. Soak for 20 minutes, using the body brush to stimulate and cleanse your skin. Then preserve your new mood by wrapping up in a fluffy towel and relaxing with your journal or a good read.

MUST HAVES

- 4 chamomile teabags
- 5 to 7 sprigs fresh lavender
- 4 tablespoons honey
- 4 cups water
- 4 cups fresh milk
- body brush or loofah

"A bath is like a decompression chamber—better than closing your bedroom door and turning on the TV to chill out."

—Alix Zink, Grand Floridian Spa & Health Club

✶ **Keep your cool.** Resist the urge to take a steaming hot bath, as a tub that is too hot can leave you more tired than refreshed. Water at between 90 and 100 degrees is the optimal temperature for releasing impurities and absorbing the healing benefits of the herbs. (Raid the medicine cabinet for a thermometer to get it just right.)

✶ **Sun soak.** After a day outside, soothe a sunburn by using echinacea tea instead of chamomile. To moisturize and help prevent peeling, add 1/2 cup of aloe vera gel to the tub, too.

Hot Cocoa Dip

If freshly baked brownies make you swoon, envelop your whole body in this decadent soak. Chocolate is packed with anti-oxidants, which have been said to help protect the skin from pollution and sun damage. With the mood-lifting scent of cocoa and a trio of soothing ingredients, this delectable tub satisfies your craving for a sweet escape.

inspiration

Choc-A-Licious

TEENS TOO DAY SPA
RALEIGH, NC

Here's a fancy new way to satisfy that chocolate fix: the Teens Too Choc-A-Licious wrap. In this delectable treatment, teens are first dry-brushed to slough off dead skin cells and increase circulation. After the skin is prepped, they are painted from head to toe with a rich chocolate body masque, which includes wild yam to condition the skin, and smooth and tone the body. The next step is a snug wrap in a heated blanket, which activates the masque. After 20 minutes of sweet aromas and total body warmth, the blanket is removed and the masque washed away. A moisturizer containing chocolate, willow, and aloe is applied for added hydration, leaving you looking and smelling irresistible.

Teens Too Day Spa

✳ **Re-treat.** This bath is all about creating a total sensory experience, so go all out. Place a bowl of chocolates tubside, put on your favorite music, and surround yourself with tea-light candles.

Here's How...

1. Combine all ingredients in a bowl, stirring until well mixed.
2. Draw a warm bath, gradually pouring the mixture under the faucet so the water gets frothy.
3. Step in and soak for 20 minutes as the milk and Epsom salts gently soften and exfoliate your skin. Let the delicious scent of chocolate wash over you from head to toe.
4. Rinse off thoroughly under the shower afterward, using the brush or loofah to stimulate your skin and sweep away any cocoa residue.

MUST HAVES

- 1/8 cup unsweetened cocoa powder
- 1/8 cup powdered milk
- 1/4 cup Epsom salts
- 1 tablespoon baking soda
- 1 tablespoon cornstarch
- body brush or loofah

"We all know how fattening chocolate can be when we eat it, but when applied topically, it actually aids in toning and conditioning the skin."

—Angela Padgett, president, Teens Too Day Spa

✶ **Lavender twist.** As any chef will tell you, lavender is the perfect accompaniment for chocolate. It's also the world's most soothing scent, so add a handful of fresh sprigs or a few drops of lavender essential oil to the mix.

Feet ReTreat

Pounding the pavement, pointy-toed shoes...where is the love? Take time out to reward those under-appreciated feet with the attention they deserve. This tootsie technique goes straight to the source of stress by targeting pressure points that help you unwind. The massage oil is also pedi-perfect, incorporating cloves as a natural antiseptic. Who knew feet could be so sweet?

inspiration

Flavor of the Month Foot Massage

RUSH! EXPRESS SALON & SPA BAR
GAMBRILLS, MD

At Rush!, teens get in step with the Flavor of the Month Foot Massage. Tired toes and lethargic legs are bathed in warm water, then rubbed and soothed with exfoliating scrubs and lotions. In addition to its signature creamy avocado mixture, the spa features new exfoliating formulas each month—sugar and walnut, apple pie à la mode, and mango lavender, to name just a few of the tempting fragrances. Moisturized and invigorated, tootsies are finally treated to a luxurious pedicure. Pick a polish and put your best foot forward!

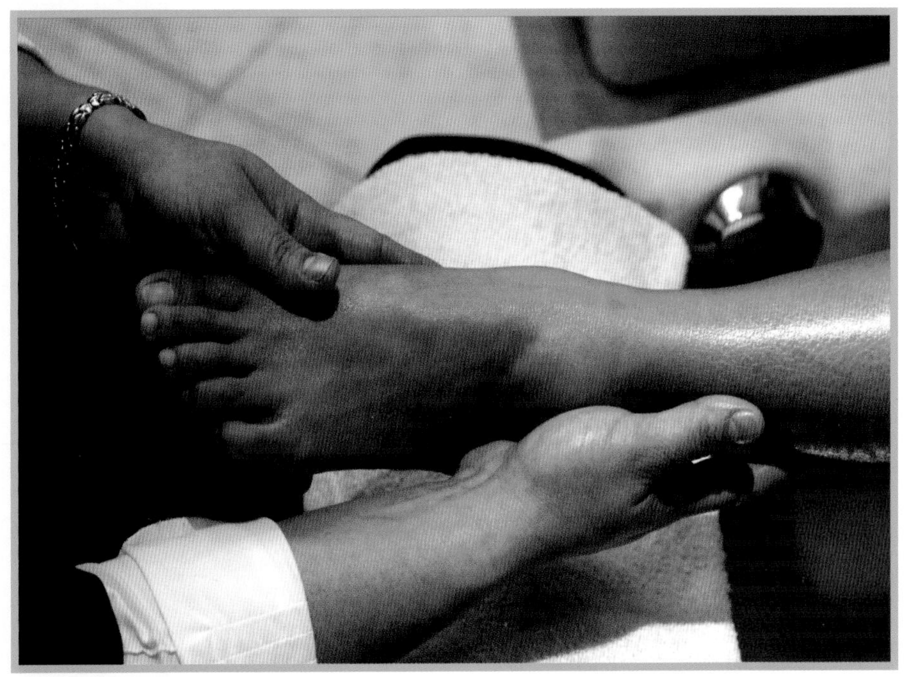

Rush! Express Salon & Spa Bar

✳ **Minty fresh.** Nothing revives tired toes like the tingly effects of mint. For an instant lift, add 5 drops of mint essential oil to the foot-rub recipe above.

Here's How...

MUST HAVES

- 1/4 cup + 1 tablespoon sesame or macadamia nut oil
- 3 whole cloves
- towel
- large bowl (or the tub)
- mellow mood music

1. Pour 1 tablespoon of oil in a bowl with the cloves. Let soak overnight to infuse the oil with the essence of the cloves. (Hint: To skip this step, you can also buy pre-made clove oil from most pharmacies.)
2. Add the rest of the oil and mix together well.
3. Sit in a chair and soak your feet for 5 minutes in a large bowl (or bathtub) filled halfway with warm, soapy water. Pat dry thoroughly.
4. Cover your lap with the towel. Bring your left foot up to rest on your right thigh. Massage some of the oil over your foot, so your hands glide easily.
5. Starting with the big toe, grasp each toe in turn firmly and work it back and forth and from side to side. Gently extend the toe out to the left and away from the ball of your foot. Then use your fingers to apply pressure for a few seconds between each toe.
6. Grasp all five toes in your right hand and gently bend them backward. Hold for 5 seconds, then bend them in the opposite direction and hold. Repeat 3 times.
7. Use your right thumb to apply pressure to the sole of your foot, making your way gradually from the bottom of the arch to just below the big toe. Repeat 5 times.
8. Make a fist with your right hand and press the knuckles into the sole, moving back and forth from heel to toe. Repeat 5 times.
9. Press and roll both thumbs over the ball of your foot, focusing the pressure in the small space between the bones.
10. Switch feet and repeat. (Hint: Wash feet thoroughly before you try to walk around, so you don't go slip-sliding away.)

✶ **Don't sweat it.** Athlete's foot (itchy, flaky skin between the toes) can strike when moisture gets trapped between the toes. For a quick cure, add 10 drops of geranium oil (available at most pharmacies) to the recipe above.

Deep De-Stress

Pop quizzes. Cell phones. Curfews. When the stress-inducing combo of school, friends, and parents has your stomach all in knots, try this anti-tension technique. While it may seem illogical, muscles that have been tightly engaged or squeezed can relax more deeply afterward. By following a series of calming and centering exercises, flexing and relaxing the muscles, your mind and body will find their way to total relaxation.

inspiration

Progressive Relaxation

THE SPA AT NORWICH INN
NORWICH, CT

The Norwich Inn's Progressive Relaxation leaves your body feeling stretched and your mind rested. First, simple stretching exercises release tension in the muscles and prepare the entire body for relaxation. Breathing exercises then encourage teens to focus their mind and forget about everyday problems. The progressive relaxation exercises that follow involve flexing and relaxing each part of the body, starting at the feet, and moving up to the head. Lastly, visualization of a favorite place or situation ushers in a state of calm. A discussion follows, as everyone relaxes and talks about their experiences. It's a simple and effective way to banish bad vibes and get the mind focused on the positive.

The Spa at Norwich Inn

✶ **Body scan.** Afterward, take a survey of your body to see where you're still holding any tension. Sometimes we can hold tension in our muscles without even noticing it. There's almost always just a little more tension left, and the trick is to release it consciously.

Here's How...

1. Find a quiet place where you won't be disturbed for at least 10 minutes.

2. Lie down on your back with your feet hip-width apart and your arms resting alongside your body, palms facing up.

3. Bring your attention to your feet. Squeeze your toes tightly into the balls of your feet, as hard as you can.

4. Release and relax the feet.

5. Continue to squeeze and release each part of your body from the bottom up:
   - legs
   - backside
   - stomach
   - upper chest and shoulders
   - arms
   - face (scrunch your nose and forehead, tense your mouth and clench your teeth)
   - entire body

6. When you finally relax the whole body, try to stay there for at least 5 minutes and take slow, deep breaths. If you can, stay for 15 minutes. If you think you might fall asleep, you can always set an alarm so you don't have to worry about the time.

"Today's teens have a long list of demands and stresses in their lives. We have found that the progressive relaxation class helps them clear their minds as the instructor guides them through the flow of the class. When the class is over, they leave with renewed energy and clearer focus for their return to their busy lives."

—Peggie Ford Cosgrove, The Spa at Norwich Inn

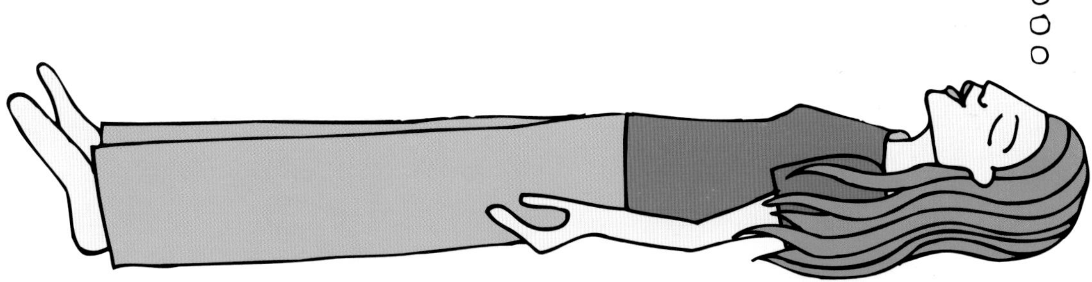

✷ **Surrender.** As you go through this sequence, try to feel the earth supporting your whole body. Give in to gravity.

✷ **Picture it.** Once your whole body is relaxed, try a little guided imagery to help you stay serene: Visualize yourself lying on a beach listening to waves, floating on a raft, or any other image that will help keep you relaxed.

Dream Steam Sinus Remedy

Clogged, achy sinuses and congested coughs are no match for the passage-penetrating power of a home steam with eucalyptus. This scintillating scent can do much more than just unclog a stuffy nose: Combine it with a handful of simple herbs and spices and you'll perk up in no time.

inspiration

Ahhh...Sinus Relief Treatment

TRÈS JOLIE DAY SPA
DOLCE HERITAGE RESORT AND CONFERENCE CENTER
SOUTHBURY, CT

For those who suffer from chronic migraines or congested sinus headaches, the Très Jolie Day Spa offers just the remedy. This 45-minute facial-like massage, aptly called the Ahhh…Sinus Relief Treatment, promises to send clients away breathing a sigh of relief.

Massage therapists delicately rub their fingers in circular motions around the eyes, face, and neck, concentrating on key headache points in a "facial rejuvenation" treatment designed to bring "cranial sacral and myofacial release." Don't let the complicated terms fool you—this treatment will simply unclog blocked sinuses and loosen up tension that builds up around the prime areas for headaches. You will feel almost instant relief. These techniques are used in combination with hot and cold stones, which are placed alternately on blocked sinuses to contract and relax sore face muscles. Aromatic eucalyptus and peppermint essential oils are gently rubbed into the face to help shrink swollen glands and encourage sinus drainage.

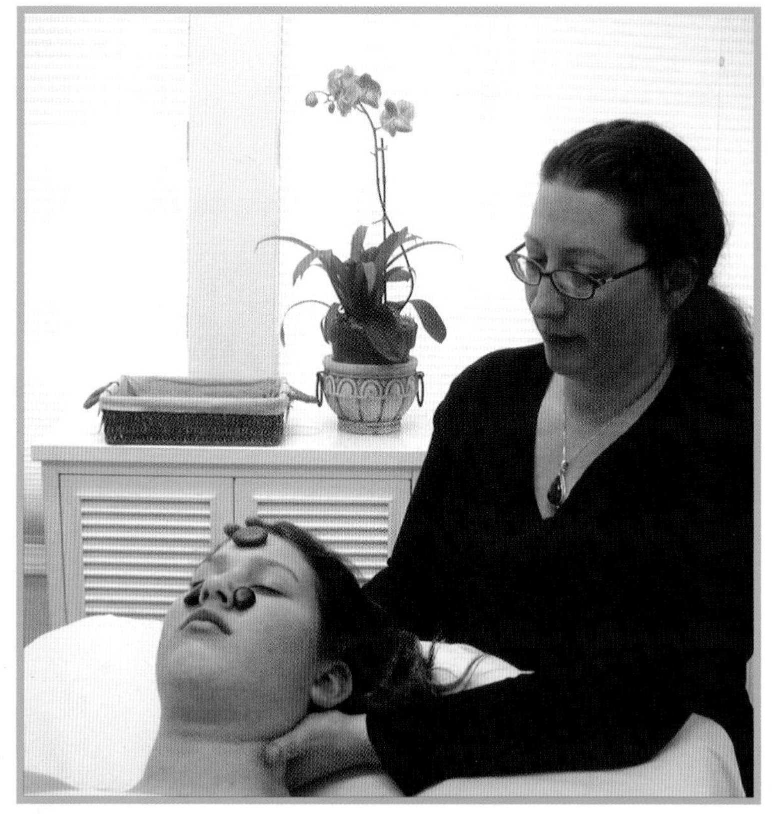

Très Jolie Day Spa

✳ **Less is more.** Staying in the steam longer than 15 minutes is actually counterproductive; even an extra 15 minutes will decrease the benefits by half. The same goes for quantity: Too much eucalyptus oil can negate its therapeutic effect. And if you start to feel dizzy or overheated at any time during the treatment, stop.

Here's How...

1. Carefully pour the hot water into the bowl. Add the oils, cinnamon, and any other ingredients you've chosen.
2. Lean over the bowl so you're looking down at it. Then cover your head with the towel like a tent so the steam doesn't escape. (Be sure to keep enough distance so you don't touch the hot water.)
3. Close your eyes and breathe slowly and deeply for 15 minutes. Aaaaaah!

MUST HAVES

- 6 cups boiling water
- 3 drops eucalyptus oil (Eucalyptus globulus), available at pharmacies and health food stores
- 3 drops peppermint oil or 2 tablespoons fresh mint leaves, chopped
- 3 cinnamon sticks, broken into small pieces
- 2 tablespoons chopped basil, sage, thyme, rosemary, or lavender (optional)
- large towel
- large bowl

"The whole idea is to learn techniques to help the body heal itself—whether it is for chronic migraines or sinus headaches. Teens who suffer from allergies and hormonal or other migraines can use natural techniques to cure their ailments, such as eucalyptus or peppermint essential oils combined with hot towels on stuffy sinuses and foreheads."

✶ **Pick a pepper.** For a tingly treat that invigorates your senses, substitute 1 teaspoon cayenne pepper for the cinnamon.

Relax-Me Reflexology

Too busy for a nap but still need a quick feel-good boost? Reflexology may be just the thing. The ancient art of reflexology is practiced by many cultures, and is based on the premise that zones and reflex areas located in each foot correspond to specific parts and systems in the rest of the body. The idea is simple: Your feet hold secret pathways to your well-being. Pressing on the arch of the foot will stop a stomach ache, while working on the big toe will help with headaches. And even if you feel well, a bit of pressure on your aching feet can be profoundly relaxing. Try it on yourself, or find a clean-footed friend and take tootsie-turns. No tickling.

inspiration

Reflexology

DIECI LIFESTYLE SPA
LIVINGSTON, NJ

At Dieci Lifestyle Spa, all you have to do is kick off your shoes, lie on a massage table, and let the massage therapist work magic on your feet. Unlike traditional massages, which use rubbing motions, reflexology involves applying pressure to specific points in the foot. No instruments or gadgets are used, just the hands! Recipients of reflexology often report feeling "crunchy" or hard matter under the skin in the feet, but rest assured that this usually indicates tension, and areas in the rest of the body where energy is blocked. By pressing on and stretching blocked areas, the therapist brings relief to the corresponding body part.

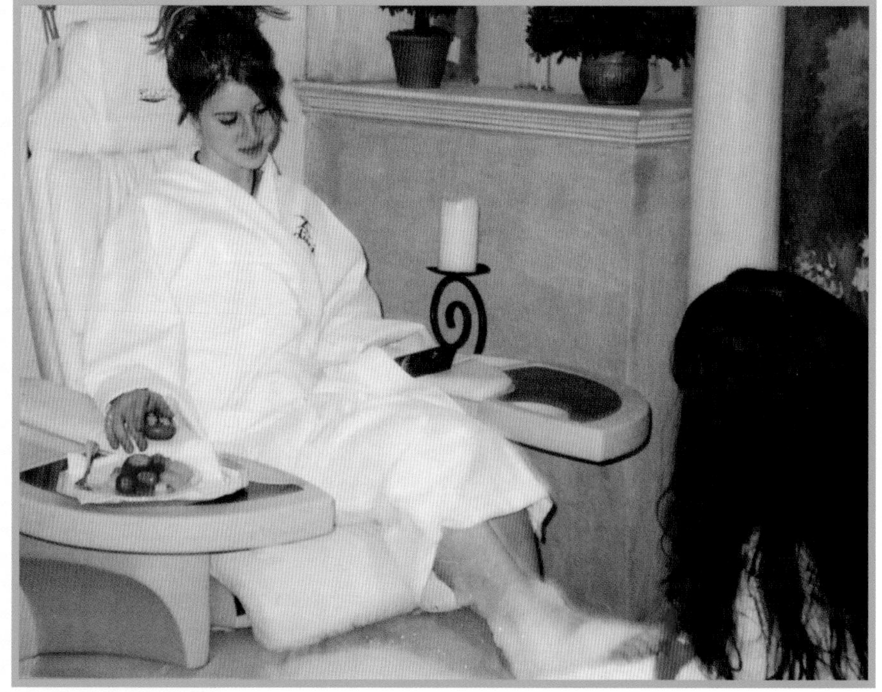

Dieci Lifestyle Spa

Here's How...

1. Start with 2 minutes of warming, relaxing massage over the whole foot to stretch the muscles and get the circulation moving.

2. As you're massaging, tune in to any tender areas—these are the stress points that crave the most attention. The illustration at right maps the different areas of the foot and the areas in the body they link to. Use your thumbs to press firmly into each stress point (the more pressure you apply, the more stimulating it will be).

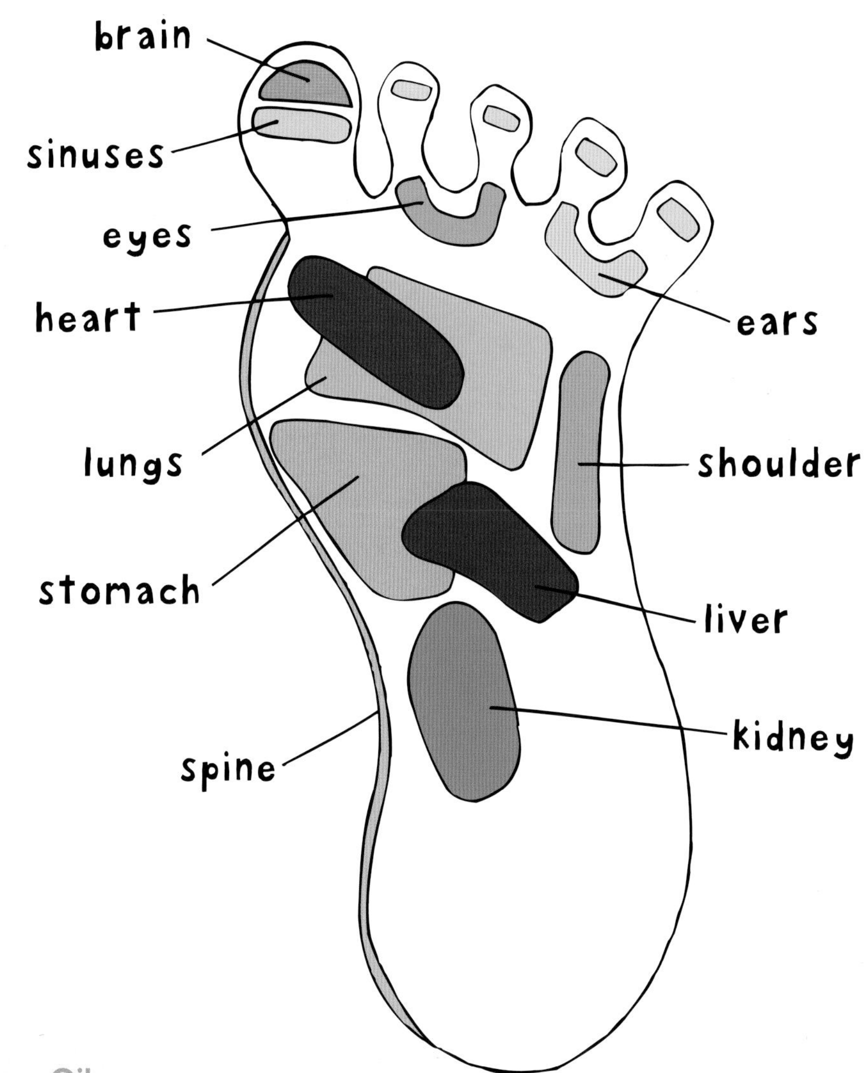

MUST HAVES

- 1/4 cup canola oil
- 1/4 teaspoon ground cinnamon
- 1/4 teaspoon vanilla extract

Meow-Meow Massage Oil

(Warning: this recipe is solely for the seriously indulgent. Casual participants need not read on.)

Yes, massage oil smoothes the way for a rubdown—but it's also a delicious excuse to create a total sensory experience. This aroma-happy mix smells as blissful as it feels. Mix the ingredients together in a bowl and allow them to sit for 3 to 4 hours to get the full scent-drenched effect. Then try it for your next foot rub, back massage, or as a decadent after-bath moisturizer.

"Reflexology can provide relief from common stress ailments such as head, neck, and back aches. It can also rebalance the energy flow in the body, creating more space for renewed energy to flow."

—Marlene Habermann, Dieci Lifestyle Spa

SPIR

BAKING BEAUTIES

MEDITATIVE WALK

COLOR-ME-HAPPY MOOD BOOST

HAKRA CHANTING

YOGA

TAI-CHI ME

LIFTERS

EN ZO E- N

Feeling rundown, fed up, heavy-hearted, or hazy-headed? Forget retail therapy or ice cream sundaes—we've got a better way to cure those blahs and blues. Pamper your soul and spoil your spirit! Each spa featured in this chapter offers uplifting treatments and healthy habits that will help you feel fabulous for the long haul.

Learn to live in the moment—anywhere, anytime—with a mindful Meditative Walk. Or think pink and go green by considering the mood-altering power of color. Take a break from boys and best buds to share beauty secrets, bake, and bond with your mom. And find balance by clearing your chakras, getting Zen, and learning the basics of yoga and tai chi. Trust us—it's fun to try something new. And remember, having a happy heart and positive point of view is a great way to get up and glow!

The Spa at Norwich Inn

Meditative Walk

There are many ways to meditate other than sitting in one place. Meditation is about living in the present. If you feel as if you are rushing from place to place, try this walking meditation. Walking isn't just about getting from point A to point B. If you slow down and truly experience every movement, you can clear your mind. Instead of emphasizing the destination as the goal, this slow walk will help to remind you that what's really important is the journey itself.

inspiration

Spirit Walk

RED MOUNTAIN SPA
ST. GEORGE, UT

For the ultimate emotional tune-up or just a break from all the usual noise, the Spirit Walk at Red Mountain Spa is a great psychic shape-up or chill-out session. Although Red Mountain calls itself an "adventure spa" for good reason, the Spirit Walk slows down the pace with a serene stroll around the awesome setting of Snow Canyon, with its red rock cliffs and lava beds.

This mindful trek includes a spiritual itinerary that emphasizes the importance of meditation, self-acceptance, and awareness. Hikers walk very slowly, thinking about putting one foot in front of the other. This helps them clear their minds and experience the moment. Walkers are also encouraged to immerse themselves in their surroundings with all their senses. The giant red rocks in this area are made of sandstone, which contains a high percentage of iron. Iron has special grounding and healing properties that are beneficial to the body. Halfway, everyone splits up and finds a place of solitude for about 10 minutes of private meditation. Back together again, the group shares experiences.

Red Mountain Spa

* **Slow and steady.** Although this is basically slow walking, don't try to rush. Start this exercise very slowly. You can speed up over time.

Here's How...

1. Find a quiet place either inside or outside.

2. Take hold of your left wrist with your right hand. Your arms can be either in front of your body or behind your back. Let your arms and shoulders completely relax.

3. Lift your right leg up, bend your right knee slightly, and say to yourself, "Lifting."

4. Extend your right leg in front of you at a comfortable height, as if you were going to walk forward. Don't let your leg touch the ground yet. Say to yourself, "Moving."

5. Place your right foot, both the ball and the heel, on the ground, without lifting your left heel off the ground. Say to yourself, "Placing."

6. Lift your left heel off the ground, and shift all your weight onto your right foot. Say to yourself, "Shifting."

7. Lift your left foot up, and bend your left knee slightly. Say to yourself, "Lifting."

8. Repeat steps 4 through 6 again on this leg. Before you know it, you will be doing walking meditation.

"Most of the teens who try the Spirit Walk do it with a parent, and it's great to hear them describe the things they noticed and how relaxed they feel. One boy in particular stands out: This tough-looking 16-year-old football player told me that after the walk he was inspired to start journaling about his feelings when he got home."

—Deborah Evans, Red Mountain Spa

✱ **When in roam.** It's normal for the mind to wander from time to time—you may even get frustrated or bored. If this happens, try to guide your attention back to the commands without judging yourself one way or the other. Whispering the commands softly out loud can also help. (Keep in mind that the actual word is not as important as focusing on the experience of each gesture of the body.)

✱ **Anywhere, anytime.** You can practice this on your way to the bus, taking the dog out—even while walking to and from class. While you may not be able do it as slowly as you can in this exercise, there is a great benefit to just walking a little more slowly than you usually do. Focus your mind, and when you get to your destination, you may discover you are less stressed.

Tai-Chi Me

Tai chi is an ancient Chinese system of movement. The practice of tai chi is a series of measured, fluid motions that balance your energy, restore your spirit, and increase your overall strength, stamina, and flexibility. This gentle practice is ideal for days when you're not in the mood for an extra-vigorous workout. Like yoga, it involves a sequence of exercises, each with a name and a meaning.

This beginner's exercise, known as "Scooping the Sea," provides a perfect kick-start for your practice. As its name implies, this exercise looks as if you're bending down to scoop up a handful of water, raising it up to your head, then fanning your arms out and down again for another scoop.

inspiration

Tai Chi

ARIA SPA & CLUB
VAIL CASCADE RESORT & SPA
VAIL, CO

Time to get grounded. At Aria Spa & Club all you need is a little mind over matter. Aria's tai chi class is a mind-body workout that rewards the soul and packs great physical benefits, especially if you are stressed or recovering from an injury. You will feel more peaceful and together, and your coordination and balance will improve.

Instructors lead with graceful, almost dance-like movements: circular motions, subtle weight-shifting, and gentle stretches that move your body with little exertion. Students are talked through different scenarios (for example, "Imagine you are relaxing on a beach") and a sequence of movements that require conscious focus and deep breathing.

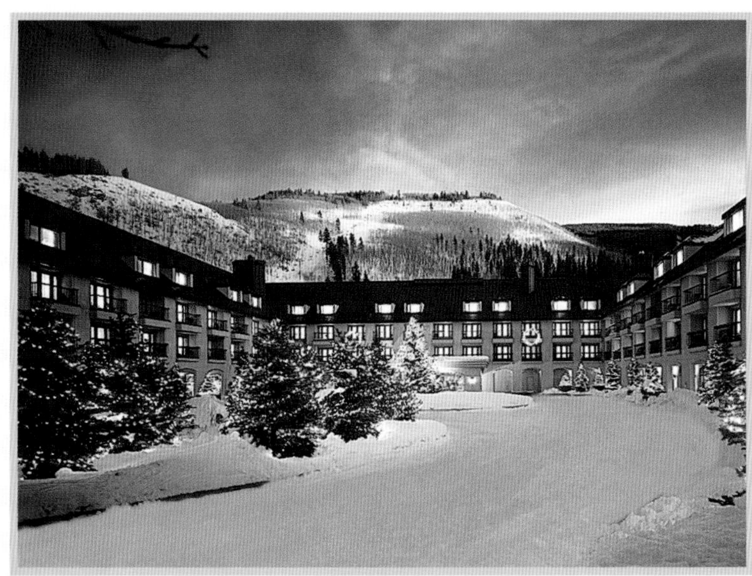

Vail Cascade Resort & Spa

* **Buckle-down booster.** In addition to lifting spirits and building muscle, tai chi also teaches mind over matter and helps boost your inner strength, or *chi*. When you're trying to study for finals but your mind is too restless, tai chi will help you to get focused so you can concentrate more effectively on the task at hand.

Here's How...

Steps 2 and 4

1. Stand with feet parallel, shoulder-width apart. Bend your knees slightly, and let your arms hang straight at your sides. Inhale.

2. As you exhale, step forward with your left foot, and shift your weight onto it. Keep the right leg straight, foot planted on the floor. Stretch your arms out to the sides and then forward until they're in front of you, palms in.

3. Inhale and begin to shift your weight back onto your right foot. Open your arms slowly and draw them back.

4. Exhale and lean forward, bringing your hands together just ahead of your left knee. Bend the knee deeper, but don't let it extend beyond the toes of your left foot.

5. Open your arms out wide, hands at ear level. Return to starting position, then switch sides and do the same exercise using the right leg.

"Tai chi helps you enhance your total physical well-being. It conditions you physically and helps relieve stress and improve focus and balance."

—Matthew Bayley, Aria Spa & Club

✳ **Branch out.** Once you've mastered Scooping the Sea, try your hand at some of the other postures. There are countless books and Web sites to help walk you through such routines as "Embrace the Tiger," "Snake Creeps Down," and "Return to the Mountain."

Color-Me-Happy Mood Boost

Unlock the amazing potential of color to bring out your inner optimist. Color is a form of light, and each different frequency—from baby blue to fiery red—has its own unique effect on brain chemistry and the nervous system. The chart opposite shows how different colors can turn a foul mood into a sunny one in seconds—and how you can visually boost your frame of mind with color.

inspiration

Chroma Bath

TOWER SPA & SALON
MOUNTAIN VIEW GRAND RESORT & SPA
WHITEFIELD, NH

Bathe in the rainbow. The Tower Spa & Salon's replenishing Chroma Bath bursts with bubbles and color, as 252 air and water jets blast away stress and lift your spirits.

Water is essential to life, and the powers of the rainbow can help tune up the body's energy systems. Combining water with color, the Chroma Bath, sometimes called the "booster" treatment, is an amazing infusion of oxygen and energy. Warm blasts of water shoot out and massage the body to loosen up muscles and help increase circulation, while streams of color blast into the pulsating water to promote relaxation and encourage healing. Each color has a different benefit—yellow helps get rid of toxins in the body, while cool blues and greens can have a calming effect. So follow the rainbow on a sensory journey like no other. You may not find a pot of gold, but you will definitely feel like a million bucks.

* **Bathing beauty.** Try adding some color the next time you take a tub. Brightly colored bath fizzies, glycerine soaps, even a vibrant stack of towels can turn a simple bath into a spirit-lifting spa experience.

Here's How...

Your Symptom	Our Prescription	
Grumpiness	Be green	If everyone and everything is getting on your nerves, tap into the peaceful power of green to restore balance. **Suggested dose:** Wrap up in a soft green blanket and sit in a quiet place for a few minutes, or spend some time outside in nature.
Sadness	Turn yella	A burst of yellow is a sure-fire way to banish the blues and get some light back in your life. **Suggested dose:** Pick a bunch of daffodils, hang some yellow curtains and bathe in their light, or spend a little time out in the sun to help you feel the joy.
Anger	Go blue	The next time you're seeing red, mellow out with soothing tones of blue. Blue is the color of calm, restoring balance when fear, anger, and insecurity crop up. **Suggested dose:** Hang a blue tapestry on the wall, wear a blue scarf, or just close your eyes and imagine the sky on a perfectly clear day. (And don't forget to breathe!)
The Blahs	**Run red**	When boredom and lack of excitement have you feeling sluggish, recharge your energy and creativity with a hot shot of red. **Suggested dose:** Wear a vivid strand of ruby-colored beads, get the lounge-mood going with a glowing red lightbulb, or treat yourself to some bright red roses.

"Water therapies and baths in general are great for frequent flyers or teens who have jet lag after the family vacation. They help reduce puffiness, increase hydration in the body, and make you look better than you feel."

—Allisyn Marthers, Tower Spa & Salon

✳ **Color your castle.** Turn your room into a stress-free zone with soul-soothing hues of blue and green. A coat of paint on the walls works wonders, but even small accessories—throw pillows, photos, area rugs—in shades of sea and sky can help create a calming escape from the outside world.

Baking Beauties

For centuries, mothers and daughters around the world have bonded over baking and beauty secrets. Start a new family tradition by scheduling a girls-only date once every couple of months. This is your standing appointment to slow down, relax, and enjoy some precious one-on-one time.

inspiration

Mother and Teen Re-Treat

THE SPA AT PINEHURST
PINEHURST RESORT
VILLAGE OF PINEHURST, NC

One way to guarantee a successful mother/daughter experience is to take the Mother and Teen Re-Treat at the Spa at Pinehurst. In the comfort of the spa, you and your mom can find space and time to decompress and enjoy a little pampering.

The tranquil setting provides just the right atmosphere to let your hair down. You and your mom can sit side by side for facials, manicures, and pedicures, then spend the rest of the day at the spa soaking up the calm and ordering lunch served poolside or on the veranda. Your mom will love spending an uninterrupted stretch of time with you, and you will reap the benefits. Who knows, you might find that you have a lot more in common than you thought.

The Spa at Pinehurst

* **Make it you.** The above is just an idea, but you can also create your own mother-daughter traditions. Get out of town for a day, hit the beach, go for a hike—as long as you're together and relaxed, the sky's the limit.

MUST HAVES

(for Baking and Beauty)

- 3 medium apples, peeled and chopped
- 3 tablespoons fresh lemon juice
- 1/2 cups + 2 tablespoons packed dark brown sugar
- 1/4 cup water
- 1 1/2 cup old-fashioned rolled oats
- 1/8 teaspoon ground cinnamon
- 1/8 teaspoon salt
- 2 teaspoons cold unsalted butter, cut into small pieces
- shallow ceramic baking dish

Here's How...

Part I: Baking

Begin with a sweet, low-fat cinnamon apple crisp …

1. Preheat oven to 375°F.
2. Toss 2 of the chopped apples with 2 tablespoons lemon juice and 1 tablespoon of the brown sugar. Spread the mixture in the ceramic dish and sprinkle with 1/4 cup water.
3. Bake for 10 to 15 minutes until the apples are crisp and tender. In the meantime, stir together 1/2 cup oats, the cinnamon, salt, and 1 tablespoon brown sugar. Add the 2 teaspoons of butter, and use your fingers to rub it into the oats until it's evenly distributed.
4. Sprinkle the oat mixture over the apples, and bake about 30 minutes more, or until the topping is golden brown.
5. Allow to cool at least 10 minutes. Serve warm or at room temperature.

Makes 4 servings, each with about 100 calories and 2 grams of fat.

Part II: Beauty

… then head to the tub for a yummy foot scrub.

1. Combine the remaining chopped apple with 1 tablespoon lemon juice, 1/2 cup brown sugar, and 1 cup oats. Add a little water as needed to give it a pasty consistency. (Recipe makes enough scrub for two people.)
2. Sit together on the edge of the tub, and use your fingers to massage the scrub onto clean feet.
3. Leave the mixture on your skin for 5 to 10 minutes to get the full exfoliating effect. (Hint: Now that your mom is a prisoner of her slippery feet, this is the time to get her to tell you the stories you've never heard before: her first date, her most embarrassing outfit, and so on. . . .)
4. Rinse well with lukewarm water and pat dry.

"It is so important for moms and daughters to make space in their busy lives for uninterrupted time together. It really can bring a mom and daughter closer."

—*Janeen Driscoll, The Spa at Pinehurst*

✷ **Keep incommunicado.** The night before, warn your friends that you'll be logged off and out of range for a day. Turn off the cell phones (both of you!) and resist the temptation to check your e-mail. Experience the bliss of being unreachable—this is your day to get away.

✷ **Serenity zone.** To make sure you can both relax, set some ground rules from the get-go. These are for you guys to decide, but here are some ideas: Try a no-touchy-subject clause, or a truce on old disagreements (even if "old" means just the day before). This day is about hitting "pause" on life, and just having fun. You can always pick up where you left off tomorrow!

Zen Zone-In

When stress kicks in, sitting quietly in one place may be the last thing you feel like doing. But even when it goes against your intuition, meditating is one of the most effective ways to calm your nervous system, slow your mind, and restore some perspective. When you find balance, it helps you de-stress, laugh more, and deal effectively with life's challenges. The practice of meditation helps us to step back from our idea about who we are "supposed to be," and allows us to get back into the present moment and remember who we really are.

inspiration

Zen Run and Morning Meditation

IHILANI SPA
JW MARRIOTT IHILANI RESORT AND SPA AT KO OLINA
KO OLINA, HI

The Zen Run and Morning Meditation at the Ihilani Spa has a mission: to give teens balance, physical strength, and mental calm. A 30-to-40-minute barefoot run in the sand along the ocean shore starts by calming and centering the mind. Ocean air, said to have special healing and re-energizing properties, circulates through your entire system as the body releases mood-lifting endorphins. Now comes the Zen part. After the run, you will sit cross-legged beneath the palm trees, with back straight, hands on knees, and eyes closed, as a guide leads you through a series of breathing exercises. At first, you will count the breaths to focus your mind, but eventually you will simply focus on the breathing itself. In time, and with practice, the distractions will become fewer, and you will feel the stillness and sense of calm in just sitting.

JW Marriott Ihilani Resort and Spa at Ko Olina

✳ **Just a thought.** As you're meditating, expect to have unwelcome thoughts that just pop into your mind. Let them come and go like movie images on a screen. When the thoughts come, first just see them, and then let them go. The goal is not to stop thinking—it's to remember that thoughts aren't as important as we sometimes make them.

Here's How...

1. Sit in a comfortable seated position. Ideally you should sit on the floor, on the very edge of a cushion, or on a blanket. If this is uncomfortable, you can sit in a chair or with your back against a wall.

2. Close your eyes and rest your hands against your thighs.

3. Begin to pay attention to what you feel inside your body, in other words, check in on yourself. How do you feel physically, energetically, and emotionally?

4. Bring all of your attention to your breath. You don't need to change your breath at all—just notice the way you naturally inhale and exhale.

5. If you notice your breath is shallow or hurried, try to relax any tension in the face, jaw, shoulders, and any other part of the body where you feel tension. You may find your breath naturally begins to deepen and become smoother.

6. Try to keep all of your attention on your breath for at least 5 minutes. If you are distracted by a sound around you, just notice the sound and say to yourself "sound." Then redirect your attention back to your breath.

7. If you are distracted by a physical sensation in the body, like an itch or a muscle cramp or your foot falling asleep, try not to move or adjust. Just notice the sensation. You can say "physical sensation" to yourself and then redirect your attention back to your breath. (If the sensation is too intense, go ahead and scratch or move and then come back to your breath.)

8. If you get distracted by a thought (and this will happen, because it is the nature of the mind), just notice the thought, name it as a thought, and then redirect your attention back to your breath.

9. Try to stay in the same position for 5 minutes. You can start with 5 minutes and work your way up to 45 minutes.

"Finding balance is the key to healthy living, and that's what we're trying to share in our programs here. The key is to always find that fun factor. There are so many ways to put fun in healthy eating, exercising, and in practicing mind-body disciplines like meditation."

—Janette Goodman, JW Marriott Ihilani Resort and Spa at Ko Olina

✷ **Sit tight.** Try not to judge any restlessness or discomfort. It's completely normal to get bored or want to give up. Remember, they are just thoughts or sensations. Over time, you'll start to feel a stillness inside that's entirely different from the stress and anxiety you may face every day. Remember, with practice, seated meditation becomes easier, and the benefits of just being—and being still—will come with time.

Chakra Chanting

Energy, auras, chakras. A lot of what seems like New Age fluff is actually based in ancient wisdom. When understood correctly, these tools hold the secret to relaxation. The word *chakra* (pronounced SHOCK-ruh) literally means "wheel" or "circle" in Sanskrit. Chakras are energy hubs or nerve centers in the body located in the spinal column. There are seven main chakras, and all are doorways through which your life force (or prana) must pass in order to achieve health, vitality, harmony, and peace. Sound is one of the keys to getting in touch with your chakras, each of which also has its own color and is associated with a different aspect of life. So, warm up your vocal cords, and get ready to sing your spirit free.

inspiration

Indian Massage

TOWER SPA & SALON
MOUNTAIN VIEW GRAND RESORT & SPA
WHITEFIELD, NH

At the Tower Spa & Salon, the Indian Massage balances the energy centers, or chakras, in your body with a special massage technique called Reiki. The word *reiki* means "universal life force energy." Unlike other massage techniques, Reiki does not directly involve touching or kneading the muscles. Instead, the therapist lightly moves his or her hands in sweeping motions inches above the body. To increase circulation in the body, Reiki uses the combination of the client's energy as well as the therapist's. Reiki heals the body by sending concentrated energy to the chakras, opening the areas around them and thus detoxifying the system. The result of a good Reiki massage is extreme relaxation and better health. The special massage at Mountain View also uses the restful powers of aromatherapy scents and light pressure strokes to add to the spiritual healing.

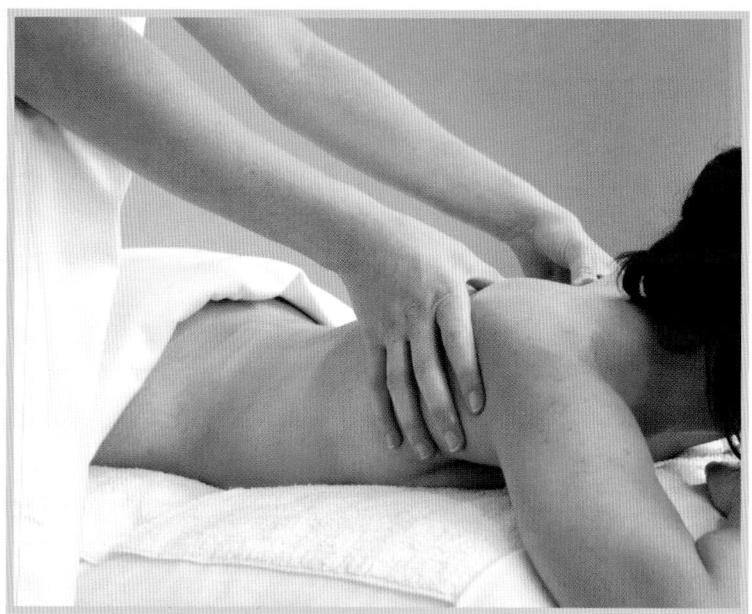

Tower Spa & Salon

✶ **Sound system.** The lower chakras tend to have a low pitch, while the higher you get up the body, the higher the sound should be. This will create a stronger vibration to each region.

Here's How...

1. Find a place where no one is around so that you can feel comfortable making funny new sounds without being self-conscious.

2. Lie on your back with your knees bent and your feet planted firmly on the ground, to prevent any discomfort in your lower back.

3. Look at the Chakra Chart and begin with the lowest chakra in your body, the *muladhara*. Note the name, location, association, sound, and color associated with this region.

4. Bring your awareness to the muladhara, or root chakra. You don't have to do anything other than bring your attention there: In other words, just think about that part of your body. You can imagine a circle or a wheel at the root of the spine.

5. Take a deep breath in, and when you breathe out, say the sound "Lam." Lengthen out each sound of each letter so that it sounds like "Llllllaaaaaammmmmmm." Try to feel the sound vibrate in the base of the spine, where this chakra is. You may need to bring your voice down to a very low pitch. Say the sound at least three times. Each sound should last at least 5 seconds. While chanting, try to visualize the color for that chakra. This will bring more energy to that area.

6. Use the Chakra Chart to repeat this same exercise with each location. First bring your attention to the part of your body where the chakra is, and then try to imagine the sound vibrating in that area.

"Because it concentrates on the body's energy centers, there's nothing like this massage to defrazzle the nerves."

—Allisyn Marthers, Tower Spa & Salon

Chakra: Sanskrit & English	Location	Association	Color	Sound
Muladhara: "Root"	Base of the spine	Grounding and physical survival	Red	Lam
Svadhisthana: "That which belongs to itself"	Midway between pubis and navel	Sexuality, creativity, and emotions	Orange	Vam
Manipura: "City of jewels"	Approximately two fingers above navel	Personal power and will	Yellow	Ram
Anahata: "That which causes no harm"	Heart area, around sternum	Love, intimate relationships, and courage	Green	Yam
Visuddha: "Pure"	Throat, near Adam's apple	Communication and creativity	Light blue	Hahm
Ajna: "Command"	Mid-forehead, level of "third" eye	Intuition, clairvoyance, and mental clarity	Dark blue	Aum
Sahasrara: "Thousand-petaled lotus"	Crown, point of the head	Spirituality, and consciousness	White and all colors	Soundless

✳ **Hard to reach?** Don't worry if you can't feel much right away. The chakras are very subtle, and it can take some time before you get in touch with them. At first, most people find that they're more connected with some chakras than with others. Just noticing where the connections are strong and where they're weak will begin to increase your self-knowledge. As you practice over time, these areas will gradually balance out.

Yoga

Yoga originated in ancient India and has been taught for centuries. The Sanskrit word *yoga* means "union"—more specifically, the union of mind and body. People who practice yoga have discovered that as the body becomes more flexible and feels more open, so does the mind. The belief is that the poses shift energy around the body, leaving you more relaxed, centered, and balanced, both mentally and physically.

Practicing yoga is one of the best things you can do for overall good health. While it tones and strengthens your body, it also has many less obvious benefits. Yoga can help you concentrate, increase your energy, improve your balance, and lift your spirits. Best of all, yoga will help you to learn how to live in the present moment—throughout your daily life.

inspiration

Hatha Flow Yoga

THE MINDFUL BODY
SAN FRANCISCO, CA

At the Mindful Body, the diverse class offerings encourage students to explore the mind/body connection as they salute the sun, stand like a tree, and set personal goals for each class. A central focus of all yoga poses is on moving breath (*prana*) throughout the body. Becoming more conscious of your breathing can make a big difference in how you feel and will enhance the benefit of each pose. Students are encouraged to breathe deeply—without forcing it—and to notice how their body shifts and changes with each inhalation.

Paying attention to breathing, opening up your body, and concentrating on being in the present moment can help everyone—both on and off the yoga mat. So, next time you feel overwhelmed and just can't seem to get it all together, try to go with the flow—begin breathing, bending, and stretching.

The Mindful Body

"Practicing yoga can reduce stress, strengthen our bodies, and increase our flexibility."

—Deborah Burkman, The Mindful Body

Preparation...

MUST HAVES

- yoga mat, rug, or towel
- blanket or pillow
- comfortable, loose clothing (sweats or shorts and a T-shirt)

On the next few pages, you will find some yoga poses that are simple to do anywhere. Together, they can serve as a mini class you can do by yourself or with friends. The following tips will help you get started.

Clear a space. First, turn off all phones and the computer. Pick a place in the house that has as little clutter as possible. If you can, choose an open space with a view. You will need enough room to spread your arms and legs out wide. Make sure the room is warm: It is much harder to stretch your muscles if they are cold.

Mental matters. Mental space is just as important as physical space. Take a couple of minutes, just sitting or standing quietly, to clear your mind of distractions. Just as you turned off the phones and the computer, try to forget the homework you have to do or the troubles in your social life.

Make it yours. It's preferable to always practice in the same spot, even if it is just a corner of your bedroom. This is your place for stretching and relaxing, separate from all the other activities in your life.

Take time. The poses on the next few pages could be as short as 5 minutes or as long as 20 minutes, depending on how many times you repeat them and how long you hold each pose. You can also add sun salutations between each pose if you want to build up a sweat.

Morning, noon, or night. You can practice yoga any time. After a good night's sleep, the mind tends to be the most quiet and easiest to focus, and a morning practice sets a calm tone for your day. Yoga can also be a great break after school and before you begin homework. The body tends to be more flexible later in the day, and you may find the poses a little easier to do than in the morning. If you are practicing in the morning, eat after you practice. Keep in mind that it is best not to eat for at least 2 hours before you begin.

inspiration

Yoga

INDIES SPA
HAWK'S CAY RESORT
DUCK KEY, FL

Yoga at Hawk's Cay is a great body-toning and exercise solution. "People looking to challenge themselves both mentally and physically will find yoga to be an ideal exercise," says Indies Spa's Melanie Stefanidis. "For teens facing the stresses of outside influences, yoga offers an opportunity to focus on their strength and identity."

Hawk's Cay Resort

Pose # 1

Sun Salutation

The Sun Salutation (*Surya Namaskaram*) is a series of movements which, when linked together, form one of the most fundamental of all yoga sequences. The Sun Salutation is done at the beginning of many yoga classes and is easy to do at home on your own. It is customary to repeat the sequence several times. These graceful movements, combined with mindful breathing, get energy flowing and can help guide you deeper within yourself. There are many different versions of this sequence. Try this simplified one, to feel the benefits of a stretched body and clear mind.

inspiration

Teen Yoga

THE SPA AT NORWICH INN
NORWICH, CT

At the Spa at Norwich Inn, the classes for teens teach students how to "be in the moment" both on the mat and off. Donna D'Andria says "Yoga is all about learning to balance energy. One of the best lessons of yoga is learning how to savor the moment, and one of the best ways to do that is to concentrate on your breathing. The same concept can be applied to daily living. When you get stressed, breathe slowly and deeply, and concentrate on your breath. This will help you focus on exactly what you are doing, and stay in the moment."

The Spa at Norwich Inn

✱ **Straight talk.** Standing is not as easy as you might think. When you are standing up straight at the beginning of this sequence, keep the following in mind:

- Make sure your feet are firmly planted, and that the weight is evenly distributed between them.

Here's How...

1. Stand up straight near the top of your mat with your feet together and your arms hanging down at your sides. Press your feet and legs firmly on the ground as you lift your torso and head upward. Your chin should be parallel to the floor. This is Mountain pose.

2. Inhale. Lift your arms out to the sides, and then above your head.

3. Exhale. Fold your torso from the hips over your legs in a forward bend. Hang your arms down toward your feet. Keep your back straight for as long as comfortable. You can bend your knees a little. Let your head hang comfortably.

4. Inhale. Look halfway up, rest your hands on your shins, don't round your back. Your torso should be parallel to the floor.

5. Exhale. Place your hands on the ground. Step back and bring your pelvis parallel to the floor, as if you were starting a push-up. This is often called Plank pose. Make sure your head is not hanging or looking up, but in line with the rest of your body. Keep your shoulders over your wrists, and your heels over your toes.

6. Keep exhaling. Bring your knees to the ground. Make sure your shoulders are still over your wrists, keep your backside in the air, and bring your chest and chin to the ground. Bring your elbows in toward your body (important to ensure you don't hurt your wrists). This is basically a knees push-up.

7. Inhale. Gently stretch your chest forward off the floor without much pressure on your hands. Look slightly upward to the ceiling, but be careful not to scrunch up your neck. You are in low Cobra pose.

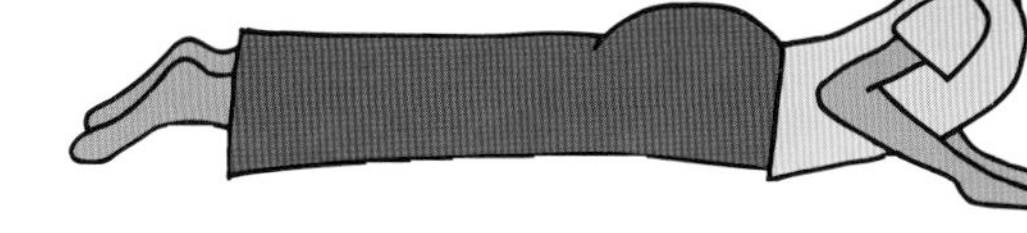

- Keep your legs straight, but don't lock your knees.
- Your shoulders should be over your hips, while your hips should be over your ankles.
- Make sure your backside is not sticking out behind you, and that your ribs are not sticking out in front of you.

8. Exhale. Push with your hands back into the knees-down push-up, then move your backside up to the sky. You will now be in a pose that looks like an upside down V-shape, or Downward-Facing Dog pose. Keep your backside high in the air and your legs straight. If this is too difficult, you can bend your knees a bit. Your arms should be shoulder-width apart and your head hanging between your arms. Your feet should be hip-width apart with the toes parallel or slightly facing in (pigeon-toed). Reach your heels toward the floor. Don't worry if your heels don't actually touch the floor.

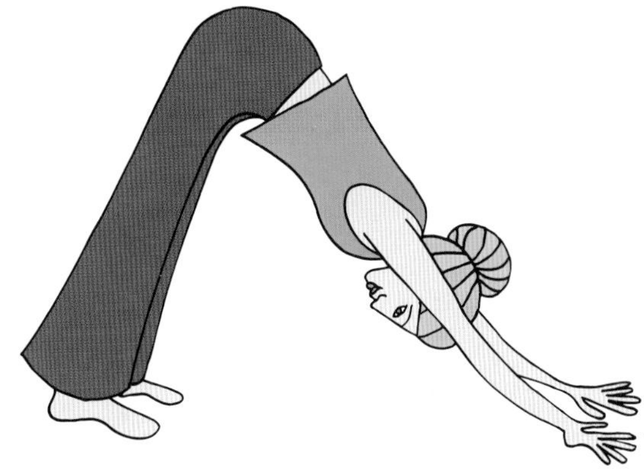

9. Breathe comfortably and stay in Downward-Facing Dog pose for about 5–10 breaths.

10. Inhale. Walk your feet back to the top of the mat and bring your hands to your shins again; repeating Step 4, look up.

11. Exhale. Fold your torso over your legs a second time, as in Step 3.

12. Inhale. Reach your arms out to the sides and up over your head as you pull your torso back up to a standing position.

13. Exhale. Bring your arms back alongside your body to Mountain pose.

Pose # 2

Tree

Trees in nature have a quiet strength. They are graceful, firm, and rooted. This is perhaps what the ancient yogis were trying to imitate while standing in Tree pose (*Vrikshasana*). Tree is perfect for learning how to balance. Push too hard or not hard enough with the foot on your thigh, and your legs will start to wobble. Once you've found that perfect pressure right in between, you will find physical balance, and in turn, feel more mentally and emotionally stable.

inspiration

Dynamic Yoga

SEA SPA
LOEWS CORONADO BAY RESORT
CORONADO, CA

At Loews Coronado Bay Resort's Sea Spa, yoga is one of the most popular classes for teens. "Yoga is very dynamic," says Sea Spa's director, David Devan. "We use it for energizing, stress release, and to build the body's strength. Yoga is called a 'practice' for good reason. The more you practice, the more benefits you feel."

Loews Coronado Bay Resort

* **Find focus.** Sometimes it is not only the body that is keeping us from balance. When your mind is distracted, it can throw you off. Keeping your eyes fixed on one particular spot will help your mind stay focused.

Here's How...

1. Stand up straight with your feet together, and your arms down by your side (Mountain pose). Make sure your ribs aren't poking out in front of you and that your butt isn't poking out behind.

2. Pick a spot on the wall or floor in front of you that is not moving, and keep your eyes focused there.

3. Put all your weight on your left foot. Take your right foot and place it on the inside of your left thigh. Press the heel of your right foot into the muscle of your thigh and push slightly down to create some traction. Push your thigh back into your foot with equal pressure. If your foot can't go that high, put the right foot on your ankle or lower down on your left leg. Do not put your foot on your knee joint.

4. Make sure your right knee is facing out to the side and your left foot, knee, and hips are facing forward.

5. Bring your hands together in front of your chest into a prayer position, and try to balance like this for a few breaths.

6. Extend your hands straight out to your sides, to form a "T." If you are having trouble balancing, keep your hands like this. Otherwise, try the next step.

7. Stretch upward to the sky, palms facing toward each other. Your arms can stay in a V-shape, or your hands can touch each other above your head if you don't have to scrunch your shoulders. If you lose your balance, just take a moment on both legs to regain your composure, and then try again.

8. Breathe here for 5 to 10 breaths.

9. Release your hands and legs and then repeat the steps to do the pose on your other side.

✴ **Try and try again.** Balancing can sometimes be frustrating, and falling can feel like failure. Try not to get attached to the success or failure of the pose. The mind likes to praise or blame. If we can learn not to beat ourselves up about falling, or to praise ourselves when we succeed, we will begin not to care so much about the outcome and just enjoy the experience of trying.

✴ **Timber!** If you do fall, fall with style. Watch which way you fall. As the foot wobbles, try to counter by leaning and pushing down with the opposite side of the foot.

Pose # 3

Warrior II

The warriors of ancient India were strong, and graceful. Warrior II (*Virahadrasana II*) can help build our own physical and mental stamina. This pose strengthens the whole body, especially the legs. By reaching your energy out through your arms and legs in both directions you create a strong centered base, and should feel a sense of balance.

Here's How...

1. Begin by standing up straight. Your legs should be about 4 to 5 feet apart. Open your right foot out to a 90-degree angle, and bring your left foot in toward the right heel at a 45-degree angle. Your hips and chest should still face the same direction in which you started.

2. Lift your arms parallel to the floor and in line with your shoulders, directly over your feet, palms facing the floor. Your torso and arms should form a "T."

3. Keep your torso upright and your left foot firmly on the floor. Exhale. Bend your right knee over your ankle and turn your head to look over your right hand. Keep your gaze steady for balance. Your left leg should remain straight.

4. Make sure your backside is not sticking out behind you and your ribs and chest don't lean forward. To keep your body in line, imagine that you are standing between two parallel walls. You may feel a stretch in your inner thighs.

5. After about 30 seconds, inhale, and straighten the right (bent) leg. You will be ready to do the same thing on the opposite side, with the opposite leg.

6. Reverse the leg positions, so that your left foot is turned out at a 90-degree angle, and bring your right foot in toward the left heel at a 45-degree angle.

7. Repeat steps 2 through 5 for the opposite side.

* **Stand tall.** A common mistake in Warrior II pose is to lean the torso too far forward over the front leg. Make sure your shoulders are right over your hips, and your hips are squarely facing forward.

Pose # 4

Bridge

Practicing yoga can relieve stress in many ways. Bridge pose (*Setu Bandhasana*) is an active pose that strengthens the back and insides of your legs, and stretches the front of the body, including your stomach and chest. This pose moves energy around your body and releases stress.

Here's How...

1. Lie on your back. Bend your knees and place your feet firmly on the ground directly under your knees, hip-width apart. Keep your feet parallel, and your arms by your side.

2. Tilt your pelvis and tuck in your tailbone so that the small of your back touches the ground.

3. Inhale, and press your hips and pelvis up toward the ceiling. Move your arms under your body, palms facing down. Press down with your feet, and inward with your inner thighs. Make sure your knees do not fall outward to the sides. Imagine you have a block between your thighs and you must squeeze the block or it will fall to the ground. This will help keep your knees parallel. Make sure your knees are still directly over your ankles.

4. Keep your hands on the floor to help support the lift of your hips and pelvis. Squeeze your shoulder blades together on the floor in back. If possible, lace your fingers together under your back. Your shoulders should be as far underneath you as possible. Keep reaching your interlaced hands toward your feet under your back.

5. Hold this position for about 5 to 10 breaths.

6. To come out of the pose, exhale, lower your pelvis to the ground with your tailbone still tucked, and lower your back slowly to the floor from the top of the torso to the bottom.

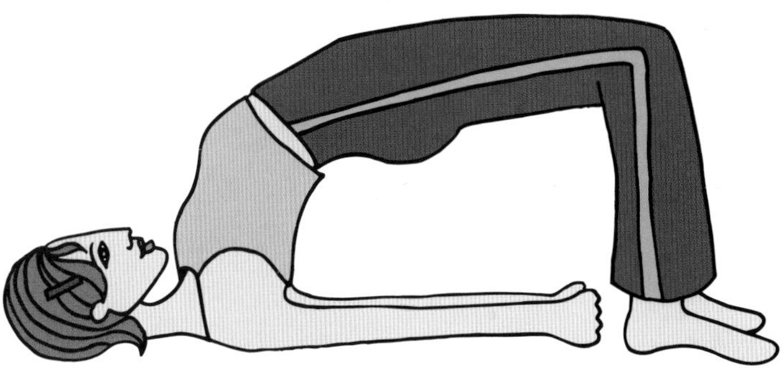

* **Back up.** If you have any lower back tension, you can try:
  a) Moving your feet slightly away from your body.
  b) Squeezing your buns. Make sure you don't let your knees and legs fall out to the sides.

* **The final stretch.** After you are finished with the pose, inhale, reach around your knees, and clasp your hands. Hug them in tight. This will help release your lower back.

SPA PARTY PLANNER

SOFT TOUCH

SPA GETAWAY

MOOD MUSIC

FUZZY SLIPPERS

Now that you feel fit and sparkly, relaxed and refreshed, it's time to share some of the glamour. Spoil your friends and bond with your buds at your very own spa party. Whether the occasion is a birthday, holiday, or graduation, everybody loves a chance to be pampered.

Get crafty with elegant homemade invites. Set the mood with scented candles and garden-fresh flowers. Offer a menu of favorite spa-inspired treatments and serve select gourmet goodies. A little inSPAration goes a long way! Guide your guests to the good life, and you'll go down as the hostess with the mostest—guaranteed.

Host a Spa Party!

Put down the pointy paper hat, and step away from the streamers. It's time to break out of the old party routine. Your new mission: an evening of renewal from top to toe for you and your friends. Whether the occasion is a birthday, holiday, or graduation, everybody loves a chance to be pampered. Get creative with the details as you gather everything you need to treat your guests to the latest in hospitality. With a little planning and some imagination, this will be the most memorable—and blissful—party of the year.

inspiration

BELLE VISAGE DAY SPA
STUDIO CITY, CA

At Belle Visage Day Spa in Studio City, CA, teen parties are broken up into two age groups: from 9 to 13 and from 14 to 18. The menu of treatments includes exfoliating masks, replenishing facials, manicures, and pedicures. If you and your gang want mini-makeovers, let the professionals show you how to perfect your makeup for any occasion. If pampering is your fancy, go for a massage followed by the Belle Visage's signature "teen-clean" facial. Depending on what you want, the spa will "party plan" especially for your needs.

Here's How...

Step 1: Set the mood

Forget the mass e-mail blitz—send inspired invitations that give your friends a taste of what's to come. Keep the guest list intimate (four to eight people total) to maintain the mellow mood and give everyone easy shower access. Choose a date and time for your party (we like the late afternoon, for its excellent candlelight potential). Then use the spa theme to create homemade invitations: Start with two different shades of construction paper. Cut a 4-inch by 5-inch rectangle out of one of the colors, and a 3-inch by 5-inch rectangle out of the other. Use a funky pen to write the date, time, and other details on the smaller rectangle. (Hint: Remind your guests to bring a bathrobe and fuzzy slippers.) Create a frame by using a glue stick to paste the smaller rectangle onto the larger one. Buy inexpensive scented candles, and use ribbon or raffia to tie a paper invitation around each one. Ta-da!—a two-in-one gift and invitation that sets the mood from the get-go.

Teens Too Day Spa

Step 2: Choose your spa menu

Pick three of the home recipes in this book (we recommend one from Skin Smoothers, one from Stress Zappers, and one from Beauty Boosters). Once you've got your plan, gather enough ingredients for your friends to share. (It'll be up to them to decide how many treatments to do, but don't skimp, in case everyone does all three.) Make sure you have easy access to at least one shower and sink. You'll also need bowls, utensils, and plenty of fresh towels.

Plan ahead. Save time by getting your treatment recipes ready ahead of time. All the recipes in this book can be mixed up in the morning for use later in the day, so you, too, can get in on the relaxation once your guests arrive.

Teens Too Day Spa

Step 3: Be sense-ational

The secret of an authentic spa retreat is creating a totally relaxing sensory experience. Provide treats for each of the five senses, and watch your guests melt like butter. Here's how to transform your home into a spa getaway:

Serene scene. Make sure your room is clear of clutter so the space feels inviting. Dim the lights and scatter candles to create a soothing glow.

Mood grooves. Nothing sets the tone for tranquility like mood music. Create a no-stress zone by lining up your favorite classical tunes, Gregorian chants, and "om"-inspiring yoga CDs.

Heaven scents. Float fresh flower blossoms in bowls of water (garden roses and gardenias are especially fragrant), and stock up on aromatherapy candles. Or fill the air with your own signature scent: Pour hot water into another bowl, and add a few drops of your favorite essential oil.

Soft touch. Scatter plush floor cushions and throw pillows, and drape soft bedding and throws over any surface where your guests might sit, even on the floor. Just make sure the fabrics are machine-washable in case someone gets a little too enthusiastic with her Banana Split Body Polish. Stock the bathroom with plenty of fluffy towels to make showering a spa-worthy experience.

Fresh flavors. No spa party is complete without delicious munchies. Nourish your guests with healthy snacks that look as good as they taste (see our Red Rock Lettuce Wraps recipe on page 46). Fill pitchers with iced water infused with slices of lemon, orange, or cucumber. Take advantage of the dozens of herbal teas available, and serve a heaping basket of tea, with lots of caffeine-free options to choose from.

Pack it to go. As guests get ready to head home, pass out parting gifts that will help maintain their newfound serenity. Scented candles, essential oils, handmade soaps, or a jar of your own signature scrub will remind your friends of this spa retreat long after they re-enter the real world.

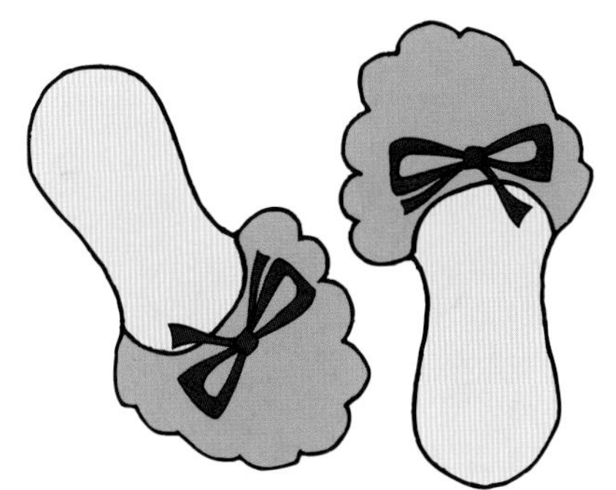

Where to go for the real thing!

ARIA SPA & CLUB

Vail Cascade Resort & Spa
1300 Westhaven Drive
Vail, CO 81657
970.476.7400 or
888.824.5772
www.ariaspa.com

Located at the base of Vail Mountain, the Vail Cascade Resort was selected by *Condé Nast Traveler* as one of the top six ski resorts in North America. The Aria Spa & Club offers teen massages, facials, and even a boot camp (a motivating strength and agility workout). Kick-boxing, yoga, snow-shoeing, and more round out the picture.

ASHA SALONSPA

601 North Martingale Road
Schaumburg, IL 60173
847.592.5000

1808 North Damen
Chicago, IL 60622
773.292.1100

1135 North State Street
Chicago, IL 60610
312.664.1600

www.ashasalonspa.com

A full-lifestyle day salon, Asha SalonSpa, with its three Chicago-area locations, provides the perfect pampering pit stop. Teen-specific offerings include an eyebrow-styling lounge, acne facials, mini-services, and a stress-relieving scalp treatment. Makeup lessons are also on the menu.

AVON SALON & SPA

Trump Tower
725 Fifth Avenue
New York, NY 10022
212.755.AVON or 888.577.AVON
www.avonsalonandspa.com

Avon Salon & Spa is a one-stop beauty and wellness destination on the sixth floor of glitzy Trump Tower, right in the heart of Manhattan. Home to some of the top beauty pros, this serene spa and its relaxation room—complete with sink-in couches, healthy eats, and fresh spring water—is a oasis in the busy Big Apple.

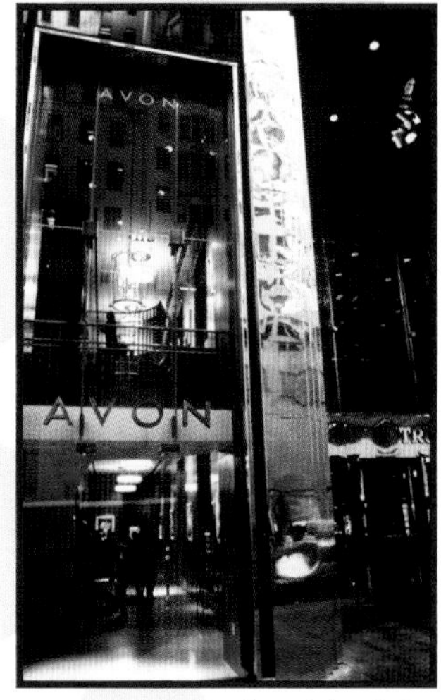

Avon Salon & Spa

BELLE VISAGE DAY SPA

13207 Ventura Boulevard
Studio City, CA 91604
818.907.0502
www.bellevisage.com

Belle Visage, an American spin on the French words for "beautiful" and "face," is dedicated to helping its clientele cultivate a flawless complexion. Its teen menu has become a mainstay for those who know what it takes to be chic. Belle Visage has been featured on the ABC show "Life of Luxury."

CANYON RANCH

8600 East Rockcliff Road
Tucson, AZ 85750

165 Kemble Street
Lenox, MA 02140

800.742.9000
www.canyonranch.com

Canyon Ranch's two health resorts in Tucson, Arizona, and Lenox, Massachusetts, offer not only full spas but more than 100 classes to nurture body and mind, including weight-training and cardio, yoga and tai chi, nutrition consultations, stress management, and creative writing. The minimum stay is three nights. In summer, Canyon Ranch teams up with the Krinsky Camp at Bryn Mawr College to create a healthy living camp for teens on the Bryn Mawr campus.

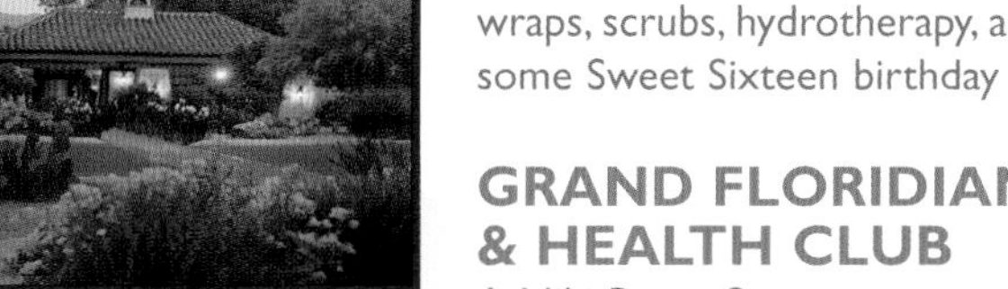

Canyon Ranch

COOLFONT RESORT, CONFERENCE CENTER, HEALTH SPA

Coolfont Resort
3621 Cold Run Valley Road
Berkeley Springs, WV 25411
800.888.8768 or 304.258.4500
www.coolfont.com

Coolfont Resort was established on 1,300 acres of beautiful mountain vistas and sparkling spring-fed lakes. It features a variety of lodging, conference, and recreational facilities that co-exist in harmony with nature, including a full spa and salon. Coolfont is situated near the charming town of Berkeley Springs, WV, which is billed as the "country's first spa" and has been voted one of the 100 best small art towns in America.

DIECI LIFESTYLE SPA

90 West Mount Pleasant Avenue
Livingston, NJ 07039
973.716.0101
www.diecispa.com

Located just outside New York City, Dieci offers teens services that include waxing, makeup, massage (including reflexology, Swedish, sports, aromatherapy, deep-tissue, and warm stone), facials, peels, manicures, pedicures, body wraps, scrubs, hydrotherapy, and awesome Sweet Sixteen birthday bashes.

GRAND FLORIDIAN SPA & HEALTH CLUB

A Niki Bryan Spa
4111 North Floridian Way
Lake Buena Vista, FL 32830
407.824.2332
www.relaxedyet.com

Expect frills galore at Walt Disney World's Grand Floridian Resort & Spa. The 867-room, Victorian-inspired hotel is known as the jewel in the crown of Disney's Vacation Kingdom. Teens can escape to the sandy beaches of the Seven Seas Lagoon for sail boating, water skiing, and a tour of the lagoon in a chartered yacht.

IHILANI SPA

JW Marriott Ihilani Resort and Spa
at Ko Olina
Ko Olina Resort
92-1001 Olani Street
Kapolei, HI 96707
808.679.0079
www.ihilani.com

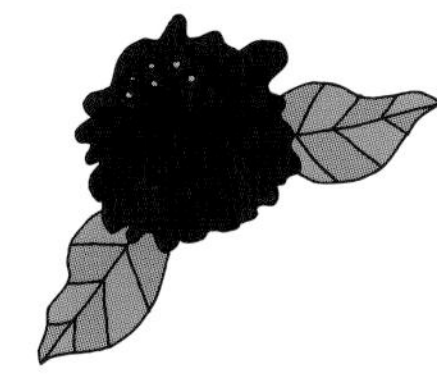

This award-winning resort, located on a lagoon on Oahu's sunny western shore, has teamed up with Colorado-based SpaKid International to create a program just for teens. Offerings include Yo Baby! Yoga, Big Chill Workshop, and Big Phat Lunch, not to mention kayaking, tennis, golf, and healthy cooking lessons. Ihilani was voted one of the world's top spas by readers of *Condé Nast Traveler* and *Travel & Leisure* magazines.

INDIES SPA

Hawk's Cay Resort
61 Hawk's Cay Boulevard
Duck Key, FL 33050
305.743.7000, ext. 1801
888.814.9104
www.hawkscay.com

Hawk's Cay Resort

In the heart of the Florida Keys, Hawk's Cay Resort's Indies Spa offers services inspired by the balmy climate, including a Tropical Breeze Escape massage, Margarita Salt Loofah, Indies Glow Facial, and a Cooling Green Tea and White Lily Treatment. The spa has an extensive menu just for teens, and you can make friends with the dolphins in the resort's natural saltwater lagoon.

THE MINDFUL BODY

2876 California Street
San Francisco, CA 94115
415.931.2639
www.themindfulbody.com

Surrounded by pastel Victorian homes in San Francisco's beautiful Pacific Heights neighborhood, the Mindful Body is a center for health, fitness, and physical and mental well-being. With a variety of classes in yoga and movement and a full range of massage treatments, the Mindful Body is a unique community of individuals who come together to nurture the whole person.

OIL & WATER SKINCARE AND BROW DESIGN

290 Division Street, Suite 301
San Francisco, CA 94103
415.255.2094
www.oilandwaterskincare.com

Tucked in the heart of the artistic warehouse district in San Francisco, Oil & Water's periwinkle blue interior feels like your girlfriend's chic Parisian apartment. Clients relax in the sunshine under a fluffy duvet, feeling cozy and right at home. One of San Francisco's best-kept secrets, Oil & Water is all about the personal touch.

PHANTOM HORSE ATHLETIC CLUB & SPA

Pointe South Mountain Resort
7777 South Pointe Parkway
Phoenix, AZ 85044
602.438.9000 or 877.800.4888
www.pointesouthmtn.com

At Pointe South Mountain Resort, smack-dab in the center of the desert, a favorite hangout is the six-acre Oasis water park, complete with wave pool and eight-story slide tower. The resort's 7,800-square-foot Phantom Horse Spa is a hot spot for visiting celebs, and was named one of the nation's top 10 kid-friendly spas by *Child* magazine in 2002.

Phantom Horse Athletic Club & Spa

THE PRIMA DONNA SPA FOR TEENS

Allegria Spa
Park Hyatt Beaver Creek
100 East Thomas Place
Beaver Creek, CO 81620
970.748.7500
www.allegriaspa.com

At Allegria, whose name means "happiness" in Italian, a special teen section called Prima Donna gives girls their own time in the spotlight. With a little solo pampering, aspiring divas can soar above any stress caused by the high altitude and too much time with the 'rents.

PRITIKIN LONGEVITY CENTER® & SPA

The Yacht Club at Turnberry Isle
19735 Turnberry Way
Aventura, FL 33180
800.327.4914
www.pritikin.com

Set in a tropical paradise and surrounded by championship golf courses, Pritikin offers more than 20 life-transforming classes each day, including highly personalized exercise classes, nutrition workshops in "real world" skills like healthy restaurant eating, a private ocean beach club, 6 gourmet meals and snacks daily, and 75 deluxe rooms, all with spectacular water views. Minimum stay is 7 days. Teens are welcome at all times, but in summer, Pritikin offers a healthy living camp for teens, children, and parents called the Pritikin Family Program.

RED MOUNTAIN SPA

1275 East Red Mountain Circle
Ivins, UT 84738
800.407.3002
www.redmountainspa.com

Red Mountain Spa has an excellent outdoor fitness program in one of the nation's most majestic settings. Visitors can put on hiking shoes and trek the Grand Canyon rim to rim, get wild on a mountain bike through the red-rock terrain, or even try rock-climbing or kayaking. Alternatively, spa-goers can chill out indoors with a teen-friendly menu of fantasy hair colors, scrubs, and massages.

Every effort has been made to ensure the accuracy of the information provided. All treatments, menus, and other information are subject to change. For the most updated information contact the spa.

RUSH! EXPRESS SALON & SPA BAR

1151 Route 3 North
Gambrills, MD 21054
410.721.5575
www.rushsalon.com

Upbeat and fun, Rush! offers one-stop shopping and professional services for the young and the young at heart. Right up to speed with the latest trends, from traditional massage with a modern twist to the hottest products and makeup, the salon offers airbrush tattoos, spray tanning, clothing, and cute accessories.

SEA SPA

Loews Coronado Bay Resort
4000 Coronado Bay Road
Coronado, CA 92118
619.628.8770
www.loewshotels.com

With its calm and nurturing atmosphere, Sea Spa is the perfect place to soothe, heal, and beautify your mind, body, and spirit. By combining specialized spa treatments with mineral-rich, sea-based products—such as Epicuren, Phytomer, and Pure Fiji—Sea Spa gives every client an unforgettable experience of comfort and serenity.

SEA WATER SPA AT GURNEY'S INN

290 Old Montauk Highway
Montauk, NY 11954
631.668.2345
www.GurneysInn.com

Nestled among the sand dunes of Montauk, Gurney's Inn boasts windswept ocean views and one of the nation's few true seawater pools. The inn's Sea Water Spa specializes in thalasso therapy, which has been long recognized in Europe for promoting healing and well-being by using seawater and marine products in a natural marine environment.

The Spa at Camelback Inn

SEVENTEEN STUDIO SPA SALON

3645 Dallas Parkway, Suite 501
Plano, TX 75093
469.361.0017
www.seventeenspa.com

This spa is all about helping clients find their style, with hot options for hair, face, nails, and body. In between facials and hair care, you can check out the interactive computer kiosks filled with games, the latest movie and music trailers, surveys, and trend information. You can also bring your friends for an all-out spa party.

THE SPA AT THE BROADMOOR

1 Lake Avenue
Colorado Springs, CO 80906
719.577.5770
www.broadmoor.com

Known as the "grande dame of the Rockies," the Broadmoor resort has long been a vacation destination for presidents, statesmen, entertainers, and athletes. Pampering and teen services galore include mom-and-daughter yoga and synchronized swimming.

THE SPA AT CAMELBACK INN

A JW Marriott Resort & Spa
5402 East Lincoln Drive
Scottsdale, AZ 85253
480.596.7040
www.camelbackinn.com

One of the first resorts in the Valley of the Sun, Camelback Inn is a popular choice for students of nearby Arizona State University and their parents on family weekends. With Turkish steam rooms, a Finnish sauna, hair and nail salons, Pilates, yoga, hikes into Havasu Canyon, and private poolside cabanas, there's plenty of pampering for both generations.

THE SPA AT THE CAPE CODDER RESORT

1225 Iyanough Road
Route 132 & Bearse's Way
Hyannis, MA 02601
508.771.3000
www.capecodderresort.com

The Cape Codder spa features milk chocolate pedicures and massages just for teens. But the big draw is the 8,200-square-foot wave pool, with 2-foot waves and an 80-foot-high water slide. At night, there's a huge movie screen for flicks on the beach.

SPA AT THE DEL

Hotel del Coronado
1500 Orange Avenue
Coronado, CA 92118
619.522.8100
www.hoteldel.com

The Hotel Del's Coast Club Teen Lounge has its own menu, video games, pool table, and computers. College-age helpers organize moonlight beach volleyball, kayaking, surfing, yoga, and other cool stuff to do without your parents. Built in 1888 and a National Historic Landmark, the Del was chosen by *USA Today* as one of the world's top 10 resorts.

Hotel del Coronado

THE SPA AT NORWICH INN

607 West Thames Street
Norwich, CT 06360
800.ASK.4.SPA
www.thespaatnorwichinn.com

This historic New England country inn has always been a luxury hideaway, but now its award-winning spa is introducing an all-new menu of lavish treats. Besides the traditional scrubs and massages, choices include nature-themed indulgences like the Norwich Native Flower Wrap, vitamin wraps, hydrotherapies, and revitalizing mind/body/spirit energy work.

Every effort has been made to ensure the accuracy of the information provided. All treatments, menus, and other information are subject to change. For the most updated information contact the spa.

THE SPA AT PINEHURST

Pinehurst Resort
1 Carolina Vista Drive
Village of Pinehurst, NC 28374
www.pinehurst.com

Pinehurst has a spa experience for all ages—one for younger kids ages 6 to 11, and a program dedicated to teens, which offers a lot more than just twinkling toes. There are makeup lessons, skincare, a teen tune-up fitness training session, a Friends Forever spa party package, a lap pool, and 40 kinds of body treatments.

Pinehurst Resort

THE SPAHHHT YOUTH SPA

Hyatt Regency Hill Country Resort and Spa
9800 Hyatt Resort Drive
San Antonio, TX 78251
210.767.5577
www.hillcountry.hyatt.com

A funky-meets-fancy spa just for teens, SPAhhhT is a spiffy hangout with an extensive menu of treatments including the Girlie-Girl Facial, Face It! for Guys, Sole Mate pedicures, and Do-the-Do dress-up hair. Outside, there are nature trails, bike riding, and the 950-foot long Ramblin' River.

TEENSPA

Mall of America
Bloomington, MN 55425
952.854.0388
www.teenspa.biz

TeenSpa, a teen-friendly oasis in the giant Mall of America, is a spin-off of the Day Spa in nearby Edina and offers facials, manicures, massages, and body treatments. A haven and hangout, it's a great place to chill out with friends or to get some quiet pampering time alone.

TEENS TOO DAY SPA

8441 Briar Creek Parkway
Raleigh, NC 27617
919.870.0700
www.teenstoospa.com

Teens Too is North Carolina's first day spa specifically for teens and tweens. Whether going solo or with your friends, you'll be treated to a full range of spa services. As you go, you'll earn Spa Dollars that can be redeemed for all kinds of stuff.

TIFFANI KIM INSTITUTE

310 West Superior Street
Chicago, IL 60610
312.260.9000

800 North Michigan Avenue, 7th floor
Chicago, IL 60611
312.239.4036

www.tiffanikiminstitute.com

Known as one of the hippest spas in Chicago, Tiffani Kim has a mystical feel, with trickling waterfalls and a meditation room. In addition to specialized facials, teens can book manicures, pedicures, make-up consultations, and nutritional counseling.

TOPNOTCH RESORT AND SPA

4000 Mountain Road
Stowe, VT 05672
802.253.8585 or 800.451.8686
www.topnotchresort.com

The 120-acre Topnotch Resort and Spa draws teens and their families to the Green Mountains of Vermont for downhill and cross-country skiing, indoor and outdoor tennis, and tons of spa offerings, from tai chi and meditation to facials and massages. A high-speed, eight-passenger gondola is a big hit at Mount Mansfield winter and summer. Spa employees say the resort is a popular spot for celebs, especially extreme sports types.

TOWER SPA & SALON

Mountain View Grand
Mountain View Road
Whitefield, NH 03598
800.438.3017
www.mountainviewsparesort.com

The hip new Tower Spa at the Mountain View Grand has received rave reviews for its Japanese bath, perched in an observation tower with spectacular views of New Hampshire's White Mountains. One of the first spas to cater to teens, it has unique treatments like head-to-toe makeovers and soothing aromatherapy. The resort's Jumpin' Jack Frost's Nordic Center offers ice-skating, snow-tubing, snowshoeing, cross-country skiing, and dog-sled rides.

TRÈS JOLIE DAY SPA

Dolce Heritage Resort and Conference Center
522 Heritage Road
Southbury, CT 06488
203.264.0515
www.tresjoliespa.com

Très Jolie is a full-service day spa located in the hills of Connecticut. Its extensive menu of pampering treats includes facials, massages, body treatments, and hydrotherapy, as well as outdoor activities such as tennis, golf, mountain biking, volleyball, and jogging.

Want more information?
Check out these web sites to find a spa in your area.

Spa Finders:
www.spafinders.com

International Spa Association (ISPA):
www.experienceispa.com

The Day Spa Association:
www.dayspaassociation.com

The Spa Association (SPAA):
www.thespaassociation.com

Index

Contributors

Mary Beth Sammons is a journalist, author, and marketing professional. Her writing appears regularly in the *Chicago Tribune*, *Family Circle,* and a variety of leading business and consumer publications. She lives and works in Chicago.

Samantha Moss is a freelance writer and editor who loves a great massage. She is the author of *Pottery Barn Flowers*, and a contributing editor to the Pottery Barn Design Library. Samantha is based in Oakland, California, where she lives with her husband and a cockapoo named Bella.

Azadeh Houshyar is a designer and illustrator based in New York City. A self-confessed book junkie, she is happily working on several other projects with adult trade and children's book publishers. Primary colors are a passion, as are tulips and being alive.

Orange Avenue Publishing, a bi-coastal book packaging company, has produced more than 40 books and book kits for children and teens.